DEVELOPING MICROFORM READING FACILITIES

**Microform Review Series in
Library Micrographics Management**

1. **Microforms in Libraries: A Reader**
   Albert Diaz, editor
   (Weston, CT 1975)
   Cloth   CIP   ISBN 0-913672-03-3

2. **Studies in Micropublishing: A Reader**
   Allen B. Veaner, editor
   (Weston, CT 1977)
   Cloth   Index   CIP   ISBN 0-913672-07-6

3. **Microforms and Library Catalogs: A Reader**
   Albert Diaz, editor
   (Westport, CT 1977)
   Cloth   Index   CIP   ISBN 0-913672-16-5

4. **Serials Management and Microforms: A Reader**
   Patricia M. Walsh, editor
   (Westport, CT 1979)
   Cloth   Index   CIP   ISBN 0-913672-11-4

5. **Microforms Management in Special Libraries: A Reader**
   Judy Fair, editor
   (Westport, CT 1979)
   Cloth   Index   CIP   ISBN 0-913672-15-7

6. **Microforms and Government Information**
   Peter Hernon
   Cloth   Index   CIP   ISBN 0-913672-12-2

7. **Developing Microform Reading Facilities**
   Richard W. Boss with Deborah Raikes
   Cloth   Index   Illustrated   CIP   ISBN 0-913672-09-2

8. **Microform Research Collections: A Guide**
   Suzanne Dodson, editor
   (Westport, CT 1978)
   Cloth   Index   CIP   ISBN 0-913672-21-1

DEVELOPING MICROFORM READING FACILITIES

By
Richard W. Boss
With
Deborah Raikes

MICROFORM REVIEW INC.
520 Riverside Avenue ■ Box 405 Saugatuck Station
Westport, Connecticut 06880

3 Henrietta Street, London WC2E 8LU, U.K.

Library of Congress Cataloging in Publication Data

Boss, Richard W.
   Developing microform reading facilities.

   Bibliography: p.
   Includes index.
   1. Micropublishing. 2. Microforms. 3. Libraries
--Mechanical aids. I. Raikes, Deborah. II. Title.
Z286.M5B68   022'.9   81-3963
ISBN 0-913672-09-2   AACR2

CONTENTS

PREFACE

The majority of libraries can no longer service
their microform collections by purchasing a single
machine and placing it in a workroom or a librarian's
office. The number of microform, the variety of
formats, and the level of use have all increased to the
point that a portion of the library has to be set aside
and developed as the microform service area. The
selection and preparation of space and purchase of
equipment is not only a decision that may cost
tens-of-thousands of dollars, but also one that will
either promote or detract from the use of the microform
medium. Few librarians have the training and
experience to proceed unaided. This book is an effort
to provide basic guidance by bringing together the
experience of the authors, one of them a microform
librarian and the other a micrographics consultant,
and that of more than fifty other microform librarians
interviewed by the authors over the past two years.

I
Introduction

INTRODUCTION

The volume of materials published and republished
in microform format and housed in the nation's
libraries is substantial and growing each year. A
recent review of publishers' catalogs identified over
400 currently available microform collections and over
10,000 serial titles. The libraries of the nation held
over 400,000,000 units of microform in 1979, or almost
one unit of microform for each bound volume held.

Microfilm and micro-opaques have been utilized in
libraries for almost 50 years. Microfilm remains
popular and newer microform formats, among them microfiche and ultrafiche, have become popular. This
huge quantity of microform presents a real challenge to
librarians. The situation is made even more complex by
the changing trends of microform publishing.

Microform Publishing:

Republishing characterized the micropublishing
industry in the nineteen fifties and sixties because
the demands of scholars were growing, especially at the
younger universities of North America. Acquisitions
budgets were also increasing rapidly, but rare and
scarce materials were not always available in the
original format. Some titles were available in hard-
copy reprints, but many others were offered only in
microform reprint editions because the potential sales

The Magic of Microforms

On Microfilm A8I, American Culture, we offer you thousands of titles not found in the card catalog.

This set of books and pamphlets published before 1876 covers every facet of early American life and thought.

Microform republication has historically concentrated on rare and scarce material (Courtesy: University of Massachusetts).

were too low to justify the printed format. Unlike hard-copy reprinting which was then cost effective in quantities of 50 copies or more, microform republishing was practical when a maximum of only a few to a few dozen copies could be projected. Relatively young libraries were thus able to build distinguished collections in less than two decades while mature libraries were able to preserve their collections by backing up their fragile hard-copy holdings with microform.

Original microform publishing has not played as large a role as microform republishing. Dissertations are the only category of material which have been produced in large numbers each year for several years. Most of the other examples are specialized applications such as the millions of Microcards R that were produced by the International Geophysical Year.

By the 1970's microform publishers were emphasizing the economics of microforms as a replacement for existing holdings, especially for journals. The largest micropublisher's sales literature characterized microform as "a system that keeps a growing library from outgrowing its walls."[1] The new emphasis reflected the loss of purchasing power of libraries' acquisitions dollars and the dramatic increase in construction costs. By mid-1979 a new library building or major addition cost as much as $100 per square foot, including furnishings and equipment.

Another area of micropublishing has emerged recently, one that might be characterized as "utility" or "convenience" publishing. Collections of materials that are difficult to gather, organize and maintain—such as college catalogs, telephone directories, and government documents—are being offered in microform while the hard-copy editions are still in print. Magazine Index is offered in roll film on a subscription basis, with the library receiving regular rather than periodic paper supplements. Most microform publishing in the past has been considered an inferior substitute for little used hard-copy materials. These microform publishing efforts are the first examples of a new approach that recognizes the superiority of the microformat under certain conditions. This new area also introduces high-use microform into many libraries for the first time.

---

[1]University Microfilms International brochure (1979).

Preservation microfilming by libraries themselves is increasing in importance. Not only have several libraries recently launched preservation microfilming programs, but a major consortia of libraries, the Research Libraries Group, has indicated that it intends to establish a cooperative preservation microfilming program to preserve the resources of the nation's research libraries.

Despite the changing emphasis in micropublishing, libraries may chose to acquire microform for any of the foregoing reasons. Virtually none of the microform titles produced in the past two decades is "out of print" in the sense that printed materials become unavailable after a few years.

Patterns of Microform Acquisition:

College and university libraries appear to spend considerably more on microform acquisitions each year than public and special libraries, but special libraries appear to spend the largest percentage of available funds. In a 1975 study it was projected that in 1978-79 academic libraries would commit $30.5 million of their $490.7 million in acquisitions funds on microforms; public libraries $10.5 million of $310.1 million and special libraries $20.3 million of $285.1 million.[2] No reliable current figures have been found,

---

[2]Dessauer, John P. "Library Acquisitions: A Look Into the Future." Publishers Weekly, June 16, 1975, pp. 55-68.

but the perception of micropublishers is that the ratios forecast in 1975 remain reliable.

In a 1980 telephone survey of medium and large academic and public libraries done for a client of Information Systems Consultants Inc. library directors and microform librarians were asked why their institutions purchased microforms. Only a small minority consider the space-saving potential of microform the principal justification for committing a significant percentage of acquisitions funds to the medium. Collection development continues to be a more important reason, but there has been a shift from acquiring large collections of thousands of rare and scarce monographs and journals to the purchase of small, highly focused subject collections. Microform is also purchased when hard-copy is not available or when it costs substantially less.

Several of the interviewees said that they had recently begun purchasing large numbers of microforms for collection preservation. Even the libraries with less mature collections are concerned about the rapid rate of deterioration of the printed materials. The libraries which have undertaken the largest scale preservation programs are the New York Public Library and the Library of Congress. Both have extensive facilities for doing their own microfilming. For most libraries, however, commercial publishers are the predominant source of microform acquired for preservation as well as for other reasons. The focus of this book will, therefore, be on commercial microform.

Obstacles to Acceptance:

The operation of a microform program is far more than the mere assignment of an account number in a budget, someone remarked recently. Before libraries consider the acquisition of large numbers of microforms some thought should be given to the acceptance of the medium by the users of the library. Unused materials and equipment would be a waste of funds.

There have been a number of studies of user attitudes, virtually all of them inconclusive. We do know that the ability of users to comprehend information is not adversely affected by the medium. A careful study by Kottenstette[3] has established that. When tested on materials presented in both hard-copy and microform, test scores were not distinguishable on the basis of the format used.

There are at least two other studies of user acceptance which should be mentioned. In an attitude study by Garner and Keator photocopies of journals and documents were made available to users at MIT for $.10 cents per page and microfiche copies for $.05 each (along with free loans of portable microfiche readers).

---

[3]Kottenstette, James P. "Student Reading Characteristics: Comparing Skill Levels Demonstrated on Hardcopy and Microform Presentations. In American Society for Information Science Proceedings, vol. 6. Westport CT, 1969, pp 345-51.

The results of the experiment indicated that approximately 80% of the sample used microfiche during the latter half of the experimental period of 6 months and that convenience displaced low cost and curiosity as the reasons for choosing microfiche. User resistance could not be documented by the study team.[4]

Another study at the State Library of Pennsylvania did confirm the generally held belief among librarians that microform is less popular than hard-copy among library users.[5] When patrons were asked what the biggest reason for disliking microform was, the most common answer was the environment in which they were housed. Lack of uniformity in the equipment was also mentioned by a large number of respondents. There was only isolated complaint about eye fatigue. It has been the experience of the authors that complaints about eye fatigue are most common when persons wearing bifocals use reading machines with screens vertical to the table or desk. The person, when taking notes, must then constantly look down to take notes and then up again to the viewing screen. This problem can generally be ameliorated by providing at least some readers with screens horizontal to the table or desk.

---

[4]Reported in Kirsch, Kenneth C. and Albert H. Rubenstein. "Converting from Hard Copy to Microfilm: An Administrative Experiment," Collection Management, vol. 2, no. 4, Winter 1978, p. 282.

[5]Edwards, Mary Jane, "Microforms: A View from the State Library of Pennsylvania," The Journal of Micrographics, vol. 8, no. 5, May 1975, pp. 245-50.

There appears to be considerable opportunity for
libraries to reduce resistance to microform by planning
facilities and equipment selection carefully, but some
effort will have to be made to improve the attitudes of
librarians toward the medium. Michael Malinconico of
the New York Public Library, speaking of the historic
librarians' view of microform has said that "the ideal
conditions which ensure their acceptability are offered
by those applications when no viable alternative
exists."[6] This attitude of microform as a last resort
on the part of many libraries may have adversely
influenced the placement and design of microform
facilities, the selection and training of staff, and
the orientation of users. Judy Fair, formerly with the
Stanford University Library has said:

> "A good indication of a library's attitude
> towards microforms is the ease with which it
> is possible to locate the microforms area!
> A poor-quality facility indicates a library's
> disdain for microforms to patrons."[7]

A large number of microform facilities in major
research libraries have been relegated to obscure basement locations with spartan environments. This has
been true even though more than 60% of the major
research libraries in North America each have more than
one million units of microform.[8] Some of the smaller

---

[6]Malinconico, S. Michael. "The Display Medium,"
    Library Journal, October 25, 1976. p. 2144.
[7]Fair, Judy. "The Microtext Reading Room: A Practical
    Approach," Microform Review, vol. 1, July 1972,
    p. 200.
[8]Analysis of Association of Research Libraries
    membership statistics.

academic libraries which have over 50% of their titles in microform also have inadequate facilities.

Donald C. Holmes interviewed nearly ninety librarians and microform users in an Association of Research Libraries study in 1968. He wrote in his report:

> "The reasons given by the interviewees for using microforms were conventional, such as: material not otherwise available, to avoid keeping magazines and other serials in bound form, to preserve deteriorating material, to store bulky materials, and to provide print-out in hard-copy form in lieu of use of rare or expensive originals....The lack of an optimum physical environment for microform use --suitable lighting, humidity control, suitable furniture, etc.,--was deplored [by the users].[9]

The physical location of microform facilities in college, public school and special libraries has usually been much better than in research libraries, but lighting, equipment selection, maintenance, and storage conditions still reflect the libraries' primary commitment to printed materials, even in these libraries.

Under a grant from the Council on Library Resources, Francis Spreitzer of the University of

----

[9]Holmes, Donald C. "Determination of User Needs and Future Requirements for a Systems Approach to Microform Technology." Washington D.C.: Association of Research Libraries, 1969 (ERIC Document ED 029 168).

Southern California visited more than three dozen
libraries of all types. He wrote of the facilities he
saw:

> "The problem with microforms in libraries
> appears to result from neither inadequate
> equipment or user resistance. It stems
> from general ignorance of applied micro-
> graphics."[10]

Spreitzer characterized less than 10% of the
microform facilities he saw on his extensive travels as
good. Holmes and Spreitzer both summarized a number of
problems that were common to the libraries they
visited. A composite list of their observations
includes:

1. Microform areas were difficult to find.
2. The general physical condition of the space
   was inferior to that of other reading areas in
   the building.
3. Light was not controlled properly.
4. There was a confusing variety of models of
   machines.
5. Machines were in a bad state of repair.
6. Microform were poorly stored.
7. Many items appeared to be filed out of order.
8. Scratches, breaks and smudges were found on
   microform.
9. No assistance appeared to be offered to those
   who did not appear able to load and unload
   machines.

The authors undertook their own survey at a major
private university and turned up these reasons why
faculty and students did not like microform:

---

[10]Spreitzer, Francis F. "Report to the Council on
Library Resources," 1975 (Unpublished).

1. The physical area where the microform were housed was unattractive, almost "dungeon-like."
2. The light level was poor; in general there was too little light.
3. The equipment was old, outmoded, in short supply and poorly maintained.
4. The hours of service in the microform area were less than in the rest of the library and were inadequate to meet user needs.
5. The staff was not properly trained to handle microform.
6. Materials on microform were not cataloged.
7. Materials on microform couldn't be checked out while similar materials in hard-copy could be.

There is clearly a pattern of inadequate facilities planning and operation. It is, therefore, the purpose of this book to assist librarians in planning and developing microform facilities which will avoid these and other problems which may adversely affect the attitudes of library patrons toward the use of microform. It is the opinion of the authors that microform is not superior or inferior as a medium, but rather that the effective use of any medium can only be achieved by systematically planning its incorporation into a library's program.

Systematic planning obviously includes more than facilities planning. This book must be used in conjunction with other sources which will help the library to develop a comprehensive approach. Sound selection and good bibliographic access are at least as important as facilities and staff. Competition among nearly forty microform publishers appears to have made librarians more cautious in making selections of materials. A number of good journal articles on microform collection development have been written in the past few years. The micropublishing industry is also maturing and is seeking to offer more carefully chosen titles and collections.

Bibliographic access has been improving more slowly. There is still too much truth in Professor Charles T. Meadow's comment about bibliographic access to microforms:

> "...[L]ibrarians' priorities for processing
> items seems to be; if bound in leather, place
> carefully behind glass. If cloth bound,
> catalog it well and store in the public areas.
> If paper bound, store partially cataloged in
> vertical files. If recorded on film, toss
> into a corner and ignore.[11]

If the per title cost of hard copy materials were suddenly to drop by half, thus making possible the purchase of twice as many items with the same budget, libraries would probably not discontinue cataloging and classification of what they acquired, but would find a means of continuing to provide bibliographic access by increased shared cataloging, the establishment of priorities based on subject content or probable use, or on one or more other criteria. Fortunately, the Association of Research Libraries sponsored a study of bibliographic access to microforms in 1980 and appears

---

[11]Meadow, Charles T. "Microfilm and the Library: A
    Perspective." Drexel Library Quarterly, vol. II,
    no. 4, October 1975, p. 83.

to be developing a program for collective action by micropublishers and libraries. The Final Report of the one year planning study is available from the Association.[12]

It is the view of the authors that what is most needed now is a monograph which deals with the planning and development of facilities which will help librarians avoid those elements which make microform use difficult and/or unpleasant. Such a book should emphasize what to do with microform after they have been acquired and processed.

We will not dwell on the evaluation of microform because few really poor quality microform are now being distributed by commercial publishers. Allen Veaner, University Librarian at the University of California at Santa Barbara has written:

> "The excellence of present-day microform
> at the production level cannot be questioned.
> Forty years have been spent in developing the
> technology for producing microform....But, for
> efficient use of this concentrated wealth, much
> remains to be done."[13]

In our opinion, the emphasis should be as much on use as on storage. As a South African biologist said

_____

[12]Boss, Richard W. "Bibliographic Access to Microform," [Unpublished report], Washington, DC: Association of Research Libraries, 1980.

[13]Veaner, Allen, "Micrographics: An Eventful Forty Years--What Next?" ALA Yearbook, Chicago, 1976, p. 48.

of microfilm: "It is often argued that microfilm is so convenient for storage. But as a user I am interested not in the quartermaster aspect of the weapon, but how it performs in action."[14]

---

[14]Ewer, D. W. "A Biologist's Reflections on Libraries and Library Service." South African Libraries, vol. 29, October 1961, pp. 53-56.

II
The Microformats

THE MICROFORMATS

There are four different microform formats in wide-spread use in libraries today: (1) 35 millimeter roll microfilm; 16 millimeter roll and cartridge microfilm; 105 by 148 millimeter microfiche (approximately 4 by 6 inches in size); and microprint. Our discussion will, therefore, be confined to these formats with but limited reference to others.

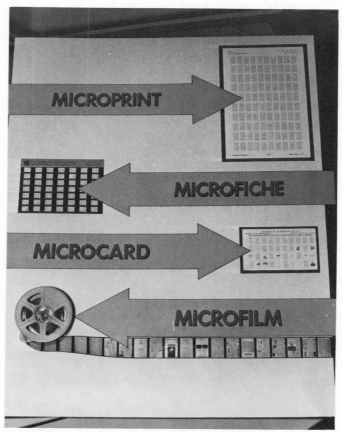

The microformats as illustrated on a University of Massachusetts poster.

Microfilm:

Microfilm is photographic film (normally black and white) with a reduced image. It differs from film used in conventional cameras not only in the fact that the image is reduced, but also in the quality of that image. The emulsion, or image producing material, is formulated to produce high contrasts between the text and the background rather than the more subtle shadings common in regular photographic film. This facilitates the reading of text, but it reduces the quality of illustrations which may appear on the material reproduced.

The film used in microfilm photography has a clear, supple base, coated with a photosensitive emulsion. The emulsion may be silver halide, diazo or vesicular. The original filming of printed material is usually done on "silver" film because it provides the best quality for subsequent reproduction of copies and because of its high sensitivity to light. Until recently silver was also the only film that could be used in cameras. There are now other camera speed films available.

After exposure to the light reflected from the object being photographed, the film has a latent (hidden) image on it. That image will be negative or the reverse of the original, thus most printed material would appear as white text on black background. After the film is chemically processed to make the latent

image visible, other microform copies can be made.
These copies will be positive or usually black on
white. Subsequent copies made from these positive
microforms will be negative unless a special direct
imaging process is used. Since most users prefer
positive hard-copy print-outs when using a
reader-printer and many machines are only capable of
producing copies which reverse the image of that on the
screen, a library may wish to specify negative film.
There are two other reasons for considering the
purchase of negative film: negative film projects less
light onto the viewing screen thus decreasing eye
fatigue with older machines and damage or dust on the
surface of negative microform is less likely to be
noticed on the viewing screen.

On the other hand, in those libraries in which
patrons are more inclined to read the material in the
microform reading room for long periods as opposed to
making photocopies, positive film may be more popular
with patrons. One of the authors has observed that
there is less resistance to the reading of microform
when the image on the screen looks like it would were
the original actually in hand.

Microfilm Sizes:

Microfilm comes in many widths, but 16mm (approx.
5/8 inch) and 35mm (approx. 1 3/8 inch) are the most
common. The raw film stock normally comes in 1000 foot
reels, but it is respooled to 100 foot lengths in order

to simplify storage in libraries. Business and industry prefer 16mm microfilm over 35mm and normally obtain microfilm in cartridges. Since business and industrial microform applications are far more numerous than library applications, most manufacturers of microfilm produce four to seven times more 16mm than 35mm film. That is why 35mm microfilm readers are becoming increasingly more difficult to obtain. The

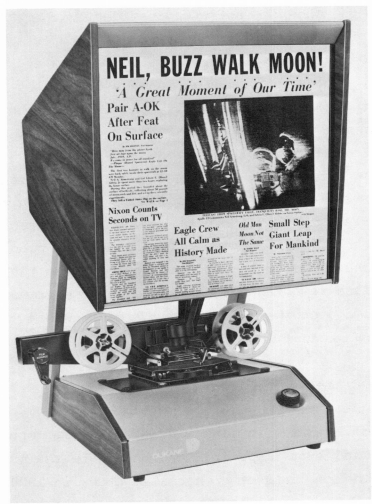

35mm roll microfilm on a Dukane Reader.

narrower 16mm film is quite adequate for microfilming invoices, checks, and correspondence. It is also suitable for filming most books and journals, with the possible exception of some scientific journals in which very small subscripts and superscripts are employed. A single 1,000 foot reel can accommodate up to 3,000 pages of up to 8 1/2 by 11 inches in size. It is when filming a newspaper that 35mm is noticeably better because this size accepts the low reduction ratio that is necessary to get all of a newspaper page on one frame without adversely affecting readability.

Format Arrangements:

Images can be put on the microfilm in several different ways. If the images are placed across the width of the film the mode is called "cine" as in motion picture film and if the images lie parallel to the length of the film the mode is called "comic" as on the comic pages of a newspaper.

If a film is run through the camera once and a single row of images is photographed so that a single frame occupies the width of the film, the format is simplex. If both the front and the back of a document are photographed simultaneously side by side across the width of the film, the format is duplex. If film is run through the camera twice and a row of images is photographed along one half of the film width during each pass, the format is duo.

Reduction Ratios:

The size of a microform image is determined by the distance of the camera from the material being photographed. The greater the camera distance the smaller the image and the greater the reduction ratio. Reductions are normally expressed as a ratio between the size of the object being filmed and the size of the microform image. A ratio of 1 to 24, in which the 1 represents the original, is often expressed as 24X; the original has been reduced 24 times. It is common to talk of reduction ratios of 24 to 1, but that is technically not correct.

Reduction ratios vary depending on what is being filmed. Common microfilm reduction ratios range from 1:18 to 1:24 or 18X to 24X with the lower ratio or reduction commonly used for newspapers. Newspapers are often shot at 14X. Reductions greater than 24X are more common on microfiche than microfilm. Some fiche are shot at reduction ratios of 42X and 48X, but that requires a very high quality original. The advantages of greater reduction are lower cost per image produced and less storage space per image. This is usually offset by lower quality.

Cartridges and Cassettes:

Microfilm cartridges are a real convenience because the microfilm is well protected from fingerprints and similar sources of damage. Unlike open microfilm reels, they can be self threading. The 16mm cartridges are substantially more reliable than the 35mm cartridges examined by the authors. In fact, 35mm cartridges have almost disappeared.

Microfilm cassettes contain two film cores so there is no need to rewind the film. As with cartridges, the film is well protected and is self-threading.

Microfiche:

Microfiche (microfiches in the plural, but commonly used in the singular even when describing several) is a flat rectangular sheet of film rather than a roll, on which a number of microfilmed images are arranged in a convenient sequence. Standard microfiche are nominally 4 by 6 inches (actually 105 by 148 mm) and can be produced on 105mm rolls of raw microfilm using a step-and-repeat camera. The individual fiche are created by merely cutting the film off the 1000 foot spool at regular intervals. It is also common to film the originals with a 16mm camera and then cutting and inserting strips of the film into a microfiche jacket. The clear jacket has a series of horizontal pockets into which the film can be inserted. The master fiche that is created in this way holds less frames of information than a fiche produced by a step-and-repeat camera. The initial fiche jacket which is produced is usually a master which is used solely for making copies.

Microfiche is a "low-capacity" microform. The standard promulgated by the National Micrographics Association provides for the images or frames to be arranged in 7 rows and 14 columns for a maximum of 98 frames or images per fiche. Almost all microfiche are printed in the horizontal mode or with the pages following one another laterally from left to right across the fiche. Some COM (computer-output-microform) produced fiche are done in the vertical mode, in which the data, often not separated by pages, is read column by column.

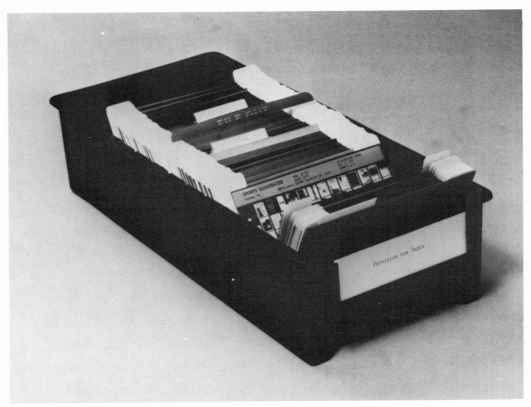

Microfiche in a table-top tray.

At a reduction ratio of 24X (the micro image reduced to 1/24th of the original size) an 8 1/2 by 11 sheet of paper would fit the frame comfortably. When the original is greater than that in size, two frames must be used or the reduction ratio must be increased. Increasing the reduction ratio lessens the quality of the image. Often this cannot be done because the quality of the original does not permit it. The 48X reduction ratios used in some original microform publications are possible only because the quality of the original was carefully controlled at the time it was produced. The 48X reduction ratio considerably diminishes the cost for film stock and reduces the storage requirements for the library.

There are some fiche which at 24X hold 72 images or less because they are produced by an alternative process such as jacketing. They are normally quite usable, but a library should seek to adhere to the NMA standard insofar as possible to make it easier for fiche users to adjust to the format.

Virtually all fiche commercially produced have eye legible headers which can be used for filing and retrieving. It is the use of the headers which has made the storage of fiche in binders so popular in business and industry. Binders with panels or racks with the same binder panels facilitate rapid retrieval, and because each fiche has its own pocket, file integrity is simplified. Often the headers are in bright colors to make it easy to identify a particular fiche series. These colored headers will not reproduce when making copies of the fiche. Translucent headers which can be read clearly against the white fiche envelope are reproducable.

Microfiche may easily be made from other microfiche right in the library with equipment costing $3,000 or less. Copies can, therefore, be made for patrons or for mailing on interlibrary loan rather than circulating the library's service copy. A fiche is also easy to replace when lost or damaged. Some microform publishers will replace a fiche for approximately $.75, while microfilm replacements are normally priced the same as the original microfilm. A library which is quoted a much higher price for a replacement should seek to have a copy made by another library. The ease of duplicating a single unit of fiche on demand is one of the major reasons why microfiche is expected to become the dominant microform in both commercial and library environments. Microfilm copies can be made from microfilm, but the process requires more expensive equipment than microfiche. When only a few frames are needed, it is better to produce prints on paper even when there is microfilm duplicating equipment available.

Ultrafiche:

Very high reduction ratios are sometimes used in making microfiche. When the ratio is more than 100X the format is called ultrafiche. The process is more costly because it requires two photographic steps and the fiche must be laminated because even a small scratch would adversely affect the image. The concept is excellent, however, because an entire book, or even a set of books, can be put on a single ultrafiche. The two major attempts which have been made to introduce ultrafiche to libraries have not been very successful because there has not been the same broad choice of readers and reader-printers available and libraries have been reluctant to proliferate formats. There also was some criticism of the contents of the ultrafiche collections.

Microprints:

When a negative is printed onto photographic paper rather than film the product is called a micro-opaque. The 3 by 5 inch (actually 75 by 125mm) Microcard® is a micro-opaque format that is rapidly disappearing from the market. In fact, some libraries are converting their more frequently used Microcards® to microfiche so that they can make copies more easily. This can be done, albeit somewhat inconveniently, by placing the emulsion side of a piece of Kalvar vesicular film against the "picture" side of the Microcard® and exposing it in a mercury-vapor-lighted vacuum frame--through the back of the microcard. When developed, the film gives the usual negative mode fiche from the positive Microcard®. Exposure time varies between 11 and 15 minutes compared with the 10 seconds normally required for fiche duplication.

The larger 6 by 9 inch Microprint® sheet

Example of a Microprint® by Readex.

marketed by Readex Microprint Company is more common in
libraries. Each copy is not printed from the film, but
by offset lithography. The image is read with light
reflected off the Microprint ® rather than with light
transmitted through the image as in the case of
microfilm and microfiche. The making of paper copies
in the library is, therefore, somewhat of a problem.
This will be discussed later.

Choice of Format:

As recently as the mid-1970's libraries had little
choice in the selection of format because the publisher
of a particular title or collection offered only one,
usually 16mm or 35mm microfilm. During the past few
years, however, more and more micropublishers have
begun to offer a wider choice of formats for each
title, including 16mm and 35mm film in open reels, 16mm
cartridges and microfiche. Material filmed more than
three years ago continues to be available only in the
format in which it was originally filmed.

In deciding on which format to acquire for use in
a library, it is important to consider that if many
pages must be retained in sequence for easy search and
retrieval, as with the pages of a newspaper, microfilm
is best. Libraries may also want to consider the
acquisition of journals on roll film to simplify filing
and to promote file integrity. Heavily used current
journals should be obtained on microfiche, however, so
that a patron will only have a single issue of a

journal tied up at one time, rather than several on a single roll of microfilm. Monographs are particularly convenient on microfiche because each title will normally require only one to three fiche. They can be conveniently filed by the eye-legible header information at the top of each fiche.

When choosing roll microfilm many libraries still specify 35mm because they do not want a proliferation of formats and equipment. This may be a mistake. Not only is 16mm microfilm available in reliable cartridges and cassettes which do not require threading, but it

Wilson Jones Fiche Mailer illustrating ease of mailing a fiche for interlibrary loan.

35mm open reel microfilm (left) and 16mm cartridges (right) (Courtesy: Princeton Microfilm).

takes only slightly more than half the storage space because the film is half the width of 35mm film. There are far more 16mm readers and reader-printers available because most businesses choose 16mm. It is quite possible that 35mm equipment will cease to be offered by the majority of equipment manufacturers in the next five years. Libraries may wish to consider limiting new 35mm film acquisitions to newspapers, if possible.

Silver Microform:

Silver film has been in use for approximately 150 years. Under proper conditions for storage, it is claimed to have a storage life of 300 or more years.

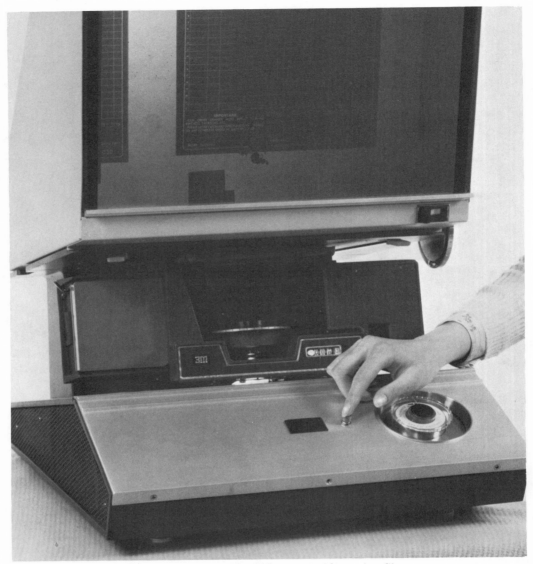

*3M 500 CT Cartridge Reader-Printer for 16mm cartridge microfilm
(Courtesy: 3M Company).*

It is the best choice if archival permanence is a
library's principal concern. Silver film has its drawbacks, however. It is more expensive than other types
of film, it is subject to scratching, and it is sensitive to the acids left on the film by human handling.

If temperature and humidity conditions are not carefully maintained, the silver film is subject to attack by fungus. Film can be destroyed by fungus growth in a matter of days without any forewarning. While silver film is potentially archival, unless it is properly stored and handled, its archival utility is negated.

Non-silver Microform:

The use of non-silver microform has become increasingly more common. While the drawbacks of silver film have contributed to the trend toward to the use of other film bases, the rapid improvements which have been made in the other emulsions and their much lower costs have combined to provide a compelling argument for the use of non-silver microform in many library applications.

Few would argue, however, that the master microform or an archival copy should be anything other than silver halide because under proper storage conditions it has been demonstrated to last the longest. In some applications, however, vesicular microform would be more suitable. This is particularly true with reference materials such as telephone directories and college catalogs which are frequently replaced with later editions. Normally in this application economy is the principal concern. Heavily used journals and newspapers which may be frequently photocopied could be purchased in diazo. This emulsion

offers durability rather than longevity and is a
suitable for making good quality copies. Both
vesicular and diazo emulsions are normally used on a
polyester base which is strong, relatively scratch
resistant, and capable of withstanding temperature
extremes.

Diazo film is becoming a common alternative to
silver for service copies because it is much less
expensive, typically by a factor of two to three times
in raw film stock. Diazo film consists of a thin layer
of chemicals bonded to the supporting base. Images are
formed on the film by exposing it to ultraviolet
light. The resulting product can be blue, blue/black
or black. Blue products are common because of the good
visual contrast they exhibit in a microform reader, but
they will not create good copies onto paper or other
microform. If copying quality is as important as
reading quality, black or blue/black should be chosen.

Diazo films are positive working, that is the
image is not reversed when a copy is made. Another of
its advantages is that fungus cannot grow on it. Diazo
film has been in use since the mid-1940's so its
properties are well known. It is quite stable and may
last longer than some printed material done on paper
with a high acid content. The exact life expectancy is
not yet known, but laboratory tests confirm a probable
life expectancy well in excess of 100 years if stored
and used under normal conditions. Diazo film, unlike
silver film, is very scratch-resistant. Virtually any

substance can be wiped off the film without impairing
the image. It should be considered an acceptable
alternative to silver film for a library collection.
In fact, for heavily used titles it should be chosen
over silver film.

Vesicular film was introduced in 1956. Its image
is the result of light scattering from many extremely
small bubbles or vesicles. Unlike silver, vesicular
film is developed without wet chemistry; heat is the
sole developing agent. Although vesicular is photo-
graphically a million times slower than silver, it
normally has faster throughput speed because development is accomplished on-line without a darkroom and the
use of wet processors. The image is not comprised of a
metal so oxidation cannot occur. In the past there was
some evidence of corrosion problems by virtue of low-
level emissions of hydrogen chloride gas. Vesicular
film today is no longer produced as it was in the past
and is claimed to be highly stable. It should pose no
problems, but it is still common for libraries to store
vesicular fiche separate from silver and diazo. While
this is probably unnecessary, there certainly is little
harm done in separating the emulsions if it does not
lead to patron inconvenience.

Vesicular film has very good abrasion resistance
as compared with silver, but not quite as good as
diazo. One can usually make copies more quickly than
with diazo film stock. In the opinion of the authors,
vesicular film stock is a good choice for making copies

for patrons from a library's collection. It is
inexpensive and can be done with a desk top unit
without a darkroom or chemicals. The copy made for the
patron will have the image reversed; that is, a
positive microfiche will produce a negative copy.

Color Microform:

While color microform is becoming more common, it
is still quite expensive, normally at least three times
as much as black and white. It is less expensive,
however, than printing books with colored plates in
limited editions and it is also possible to get greater
accuracy in reproduction with film dyes than with
printing inks. There is still some uncertainty about
how long the colors will remain true. In the field of
medical illustration, in which reliability of color is
critical, color microform is frequently replaced. The
art microform now being purchased by libraries will
have to be re-examined after five and ten years to
determine whether the color remains true.

Selecting Good Quality Microform:

A number of journal articles have sought to
introduce librarians to the technical issues of
evaluating density, contrast, resolution and other
elements of microform. Technical knowledge of this
type can be of value in determining when a microform is
unsatisfactory, but the average librarian usually does
not have, nor does he/she want to acquire, the techni-

cal expertise and equipment necessary for such evaluation. It is the view of the authors that experience in
working with microform will soon make it possible for
anyone to determine what is a reasonable standard of
quality. Most microform publishers sell excellent
quality products. However, when a library does receive
microform which is difficult to read or which is
clearly inferior to other products that the library
has purchased, the material should be returned as
unacceptable even if the librarian doesn't know the
technical terms with which to describe the defects.
After all, we reject other products which don't perform
as we expect even though we don't understand them
technically.

In addition, microform publishers have reputations
among librarians which can be ascertained before doing
business with them. Discussions at professional
meetings, correspondence and telephone inquiries to
other libraries are all useful ways to determine what
experience others have had with a microform publisher
that is not known.

Care of Microform:

The condition of microform in many libraries is
extremely poor, often being scratched, smudged, and
torn. A few libraries have begun to systematically
clean microform using special equipment and/or to apply
special coatings to extend the life of the microform.
The special equipment will be described in a later

chapter. The authors have also used 3M Photogard ® to protect microform and believe it is an excellent product but it is much too costly for treating any microform that is not used on a daily basis. The cost is $6.00 to $8.00 for treating a 100 foot reel of 35mm silver film (it is not usable on other types). It is, however, highly recommended for treating badly scratched film.

A library can protect new film most economically by providing suitable storage containers and cabinets, maintaining proper temperature and humidity, selecting good reading equipment, performing regular equipment maintenance, and training staff and users how to use microform properly.

Temperature and humidity in the microform area should not only be moderate, but stable. General storage conditions are discussed in Chapter III, Space Selection and Preparation. In addition, no microform should be left under a lighted reader for any extended period of time.

Microform should be stored in appropriate cabinets or on shelves in special boxes as described in the chapter on storage equipment. Rubber bands should never be used on roll film because they usually contain sulfur that is damaging to film. Acid free paper wrappers are available for holding roll film securely on the reels. Envelopes made from acid free paper should be used for all microfiche.

Care should be taken to handle all microform by
the edges since acid from skin can damage silver films
and fingerprints can obscure images on all types of
microform. Any smudges should be wiped off before
returning the microform to the storage unit. A clean,
dry, lint-free cloth should be used, or the special
sponges provided in the widely available fiche cleaning
kits.

A library should invest in one or more cleaning
kits for machine care. A kit from a microform supply
house contains only materials which may safely be used
on microform, while reliance on just anything available
in the library may result in using something which is
damaging to the microform. A typical kit is pictured.
If the library doesn't wish to purchase the kits, it
should purchase lint proof cloths and Freon® TF
non-toxic solvent.

Dust and dirt in the microform reader can be
harmful to microforms. Machines should, therefore, be
kept covered when not in use and should be cleaned
regularly, at least weekly. Heavily used machines or
those which are housed in dusty areas should have their
glass flats cleaned every day. Weekly inspections
should be made of each unit to identify unreported
problems such as poorly aligned rollers that can cause
undetected damage to the microforms. Film and fiche
storage cabinets should be vacuumed periodically.

Broken roll film should not be permanently

repaired with adhesive tapes of any kind. A special
archival-adhesive tape is available for emergency
repairs, but all permanent repairs should be done by
splicing. The permanent repairs should be made within
a day or two. Inexpensive splicing equipment is
available that results in both more durable and safer
repairs. It is discussed in the chapter on equipment.

How to Deal with Serious Damage:

    The fungus of which we have spoken grows either
on the emulsion surface or on the back of the
microform, or even on the film reel. It looks very
much like the mildew around a bathtub or the mold on
cheese. If fungus growth has progressed far enough it
will cause permanent damage. The emulsion will break
down chemically and will become soluble in water.
Water and water solutions should, therefore, not be
used to remove fungus. The film should be cleaned by
wiping it with soft cotton moistened with an
appropriate film-cleaning liquid. A film manufacturing company should be consulted for advice on the
best solution for the particular type of microform.
It may be necessary to contact the micro-publisher
first to get the necessary specifications. Improved
humidity control is essential if this condition is
found.

    Microscopic blemishes in the form of red or yellow
spots may occur on microform which has been stored for
one or more decades. The spots occur only on silver

film. They are believed to be caused by local oxidation of the imaging silver. The blemishes usually appear on the leader first so it is often possible to identify the condition before it spreads to the text. Storage in a polluted environment is believed to be the most common cause of this problem. The best preventive remedy is air conditioning. The use of tightly sealed metal storage containers for archival film is also desirable. Treatment of damaged film should be undertaken only on the advice of the manufacturer of the film.

Water damage is another potential danger. If film has been subjected to water, do not let it dry out. The drying will cause the emulsion to stick to the back of the adjacent film. Keep the film moist, in pails of water if necessary, and contact the manufacturer of the film for the appropriate procedure for soaking and drying the film. This process requires the use of a film processor. If the library does not have one, or if a large amount of film is involved, it will be necessary to utilize the services of a microform laboratory.

While all of the aforementioned are potential problems in any microform facility, more than anything else, cleanliness is the key to protecting a library's investment in the microform collection.

III
Space Selection
and
Preparation

SPACE SELECTION AND PREPARATION

The placement of the microform facilities within a library may have a significant effect on patron reaction to the medium. Ideally microforms would be arranged throughout the library by subject so that the browser would encounter them in the same way as printed materials. In fact, this is seldom practical because it would not be possible to gain the considerable storage advantages of special high-capacity microform storage equipment and it would require a much larger number of microform reading machines than most libraries can afford. Placing reading machines is like placing elevators. They can function more efficiently when placed in banks or groupings. Waiting for a single occupied reading machine is likely to take much longer than waiting for a single elevator. Waiting for one of several should take less time in either case.

A small library facility might have only one microform area, but a large building of several floors might have several. Each should be large enough to have a variety of equipment, including the capability to make prints from each microform format. The same level of staff expertise should be provided at each microform service point. If this is not possible, the library should centralize its microform resources.

Amount of Space:

Microform facilities are usually quite small when compared with the buildings or rooms in which they are housed. That is reasonable, of course, because the microform format represents up to a 97% space saving as compared with the original hard-copy. Even with the addition of up to 40 square feet for each reading position, few microform areas in large libraries exceed 5,000 square feet.

The exact requirements will depend on the types of microform and the storage equipment selected. A good rule of thumb is to estimate 100 reels of 35mm film per square foot (or 200 reels of 16mm) and 2,300 fiche per square foot if the most efficient form of cabinet storage will be used. Microfilm reader and reader-printer positions will require 40 square feet each and microfiche reading positions will require 30 square feet each if machines are placed on tables. In 4 foot wide carrels each will take 40 square feet.

A minimum of 250 square feet of staff space is also needed. More detailed information is given later in this chapter.

Microform areas should be over-programmed. In other words, plan on more space than the calculations suggest. Microform collections grow rapidly, often by large increments due to the purchase of large backfiles of journals or documents.

<u>Location:</u>

The typical location for a microform facility is in the basement or other available space which is not regarded as prime space. In the past two years one of the major microform equipment vendors has been publicizing one of the facilities it designed for a private university in New England. While superior to most of the facilities the authors have seen, this "model facility" is also in a basement, difficult to find and surrounded by four weight bearing walls so that it cannot be expanded when it fills the available space.

The relationship of the microform collection to the other collections of the library should be the primary factor in determining location. If the collection is predominantly made up of newspapers, periodicals, and government documents, a physical proximity to these areas should be sought. If the library relies on printed indexes and catalogs to guide patrons to the contents of microform collections and does not wish to duplicate these for the microform area, the facility should be near the reference collection in which these finding tools are housed.

If a library wishes to promote the use of microform, a visible area adjacent to a point of heavy traffic is desirable. One major academic library moved its microform facility into its old reserve room on the main floor when reserve was relocated to enlarge it.

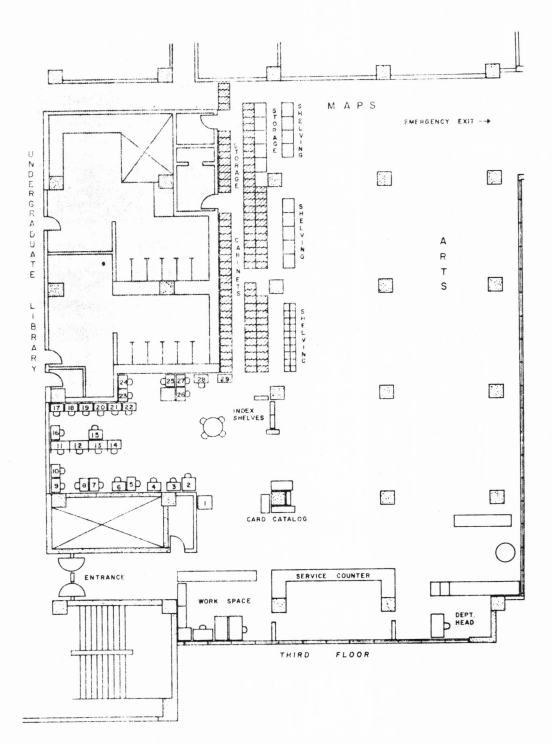

The Michigan State University Library microform area is an integral part of the 3rd floor service areas.

The highly visible space on the main floor resulted in
a large number of "walk-ins" who investigated the
facilities and the collections. The use went up.

Ideally, the microforms area should be a separate
room or a portion of a floor in an open modular
building that is square or no more than twice the
distance in one dimension than it is in the other. It
should be possible to visually control the service area
adjacent to the door or near the logical entry point
into an open microforms area. That service area should
contain an office for the microforms librarian (150
square feet) and a work area for staff (100 square feet
per person on duty at any one time).

The library's ability to staff the microform
facility should not be overlooked in planning its

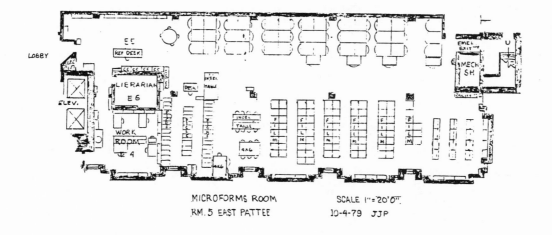

Pennsylvania University Library Microforms Room floor plan.

Microforms service and work area at Michigan State University Library.

location. If a library cannot assign a full-time
professional or high level para-professional to the
area, it should be adjacent to another unit which can
provide the necessary coverage.

General Environmental Requirements:

The most essential requirements for any space are
environmental. The relative humidity should be
maintained at from 40 to 50 percent and the temperature
should be maintained near 70 degrees F. If microform
gets too damp mold can form on it, causing damage to
the photographic image over a long period of time. Dry
film can become brittle and crack--although film stored

in areas as low as 15% humidity can usually be treated successfully.

Most libraries are limited by the general air conditioning systems of their buildings. There are extreme conditions which warrant the addition of special equipment in the microform area. If the humidity is consistently low or high or is subject to rapid changes, a humidifier and/or dehumidifier should be installed. The dehumidifier is much more essential. Humidity over 60% for a sustained period of time is not at all uncommon but is definitely damaging. Dehumidifiers using crystals of calcium chloride or other desiccants should not be used because they often give off fine dust particles which can abrade or bleach the microform. Low humidity is usually not permanently damaging unless it remains at below 15% for an extended period of time.   Only libraries in arid regions need to concern themselves with that problem. Water trays and chemical solutions for increasing humidity should not be used because there is too little control over the amount of humidity produced. They can actually create excessively humid conditions inside a storage cabinet. A supplementary air conditioning unit should also be considered if the temperature rises over 80 degrees F. regularly or if the temperature is subject to rapid changes.

Film can be as easily destroyed by water as books. Microform storage should, therefore, not be underneath water pipes or in an area which has fire sprinklers unless they are sheltered from the water. A reasonably dust-free environment is also important. Regular cleaning of the machines and periodic vacuuming of the storage equipment is necessary. If special air conditioning is installed, the incorporation of an electrostatic air filter to remove particulate matter from the air is a good idea.

Acoustic control is important because of machine noise and the movement of people in what will be a relatively densely populated area--the occupancy rate of microform areas tends to be much closer to capacity than regular reading areas. Not only should acoustic tile be used on the ceilings, but walls should be covered with a sound absorbant material. Wall carpeting is particularly effective and attractive. In addition to absorbing sound it helps reduce glare in a room, a major source of problems in a microform area. Floors should also be carpeted. If there is a local restriction on carpeting, the use of cork or another sound absorbing flooring material should be considered.

No special fire precautions are needed because virtually all commercially distributed film is slow burning. There should, nevertheless, be a no smoking rule and fire extinguishers should be on hand--the type which are recommended for electrical fires.

The authors do not believe in dark microform reading rooms. That was necessary at one time when many front projection viewers with small wattage bulbs

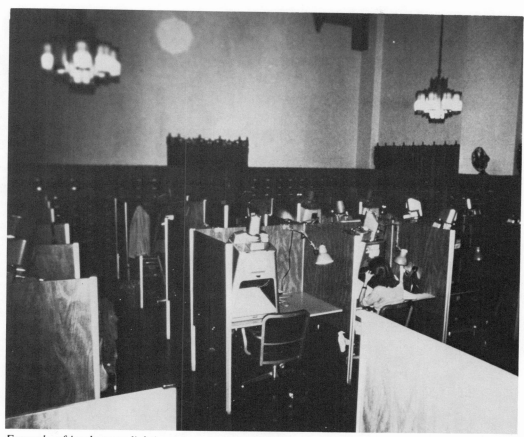

Example of inadequate lighting in a microform reading room.

and without light hoods were in use. Today's equipment
is designed to be used in modern offices and plants
with normal lighting. Glare is the problem today. It
is encountered when machines are placed so that direct
exterior light is reflected off the screens. It may
also be a problem when low light fixtures are reflected
on the screens. The vertical screens of rear
projection readers are particularly subject to external
light and floor/table lamp reflections. The horizontal
screens of front projection readers are most likely to
reflect ceiling lights.

Another example of a poorly-lit reading area.

Drapes or blinds on the windows and proper
placement of machines are usually all that is necessary
to deal with light problems. If more adjustment is
needed, a small number of light bulbs or tubes can be
removed from fixtures, not to reduce the overall light
level, but to minimize glare. One of the worst
examples of light reflection the authors have
encountered was in a library that had removed most of
the tubes in the fixtures above the reading machines
while leaving the adjacent storage area brightly lit.
The machines were placed so that the surface mounted
light fixtures were reflected on the screens. Patrons
complained about bad lighting, and the staff took out
yet more tubes--again above the reading machines. It

SUNY-Stony Brook's well-lit microform reading area.

was almost impossible to walk around without stumbling especially if one had just come from the brightly lit storage area.

In another facility designed by a commercial vendor of microform equipment there are recessed spotlights above the carrels (one per 3-4 carrels). The lighting pattern which we observed was one of alternating glare and deep shadow. The patrons consulted had very negative opinions. One borrowed a portable machine regularly and took it to a nearby conventional reading room.

After having said all that, we recognize that some

patrons cannot be convinced that microform readers no longer require dark rooms. It is, therefore, a good idea when the library has a number of machines to place one or more of them in a very dimly lit area to be responsive to user opinion.

Layout:

The layout of a microform area should be simple. It must be possible for a newcomer to understand the basic arrangement upon entering. The zones of activity which should be apparent are the reading area, reading machine area, service desk, duplicating area, and display area.

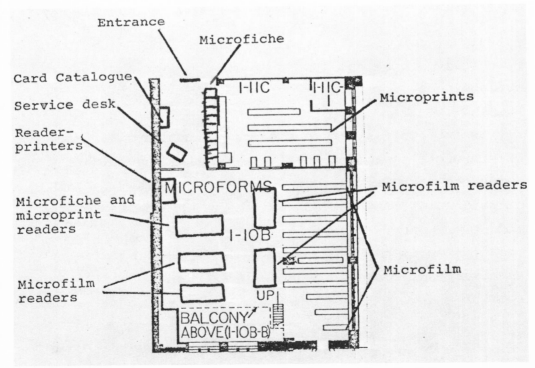

Floor plan of Princeton University Library illustrating clear separation of activity areas.

Example of a prominent service desk just inside entrance at Boston University Library.

An example of an existing function layout is illustrated on the next page. The service desk is located in the center within view of the entrance. All traffic passes in front of the desk. Most of the roll film readers, the ones most likely to pose a problem for patrons, are within view of the desk. The collection is open access, but the staff member has visual control.

Reading Area:

Regular library carrels with a surface of 2 by 3 feet are not adequate as bases for desk top microform

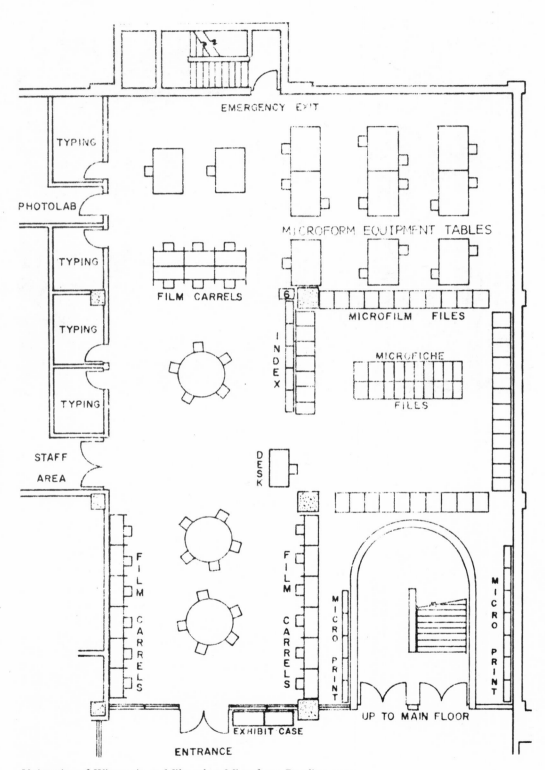

University of Wisconsin at Milwaukee Microform Reading area.

readers. They just do not allow enough space to place
books and other belongings and to take notes. If the
machine is pushed to one side, usually to the left,
left handed persons will be seriously inconvenienced.

Microfilm readers without adequate note-taking space.

Another example of lack of space for note-taking.

Many libraries feel their resources are too limited to purchase large carrels which measure 2 by 4 feet. They want to use equipment which they already have. If that is the case, long tables of 6 to 8 feet in length are better than carrels. The machines should be placed on the tables in an alternating pattern so that the back of one machine fits between the backs of two other machines on the other side of the table.

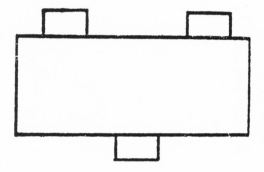

In this way a machine can be placed each 3 to 4 feet (depending on whether it is a fiche or roll film machine) and still allow room on both sides for writing.

SUNY-Stony Brook use of tables for microform readers.

The major advantage of tables is that each machine can be allocated as much space as is needed. Some

University of Michigan use of tables for microform readers.

machines are only 15 inches wide while others are as much as 30 inches wide. Carrels are much less flexible in this regard. The major advantage of the carrels

Herman Miller 48" carrel at Michigan State University Library.

over the tables is that the former have full "returns" and provide the visual privacy which serious researchers like when they are working for several hours. Again, alternating the placement of machines on tables can provide some of this visual screening.

Carrels are usually arranged in rows, with all of them facing in the same direction. There is an alternative arrangement which provides greater visual privacy for readers. An alternating pattern has every other carrel facing in the opposite direction. Yet a third pattern is a swastika-like four carrel cluster.

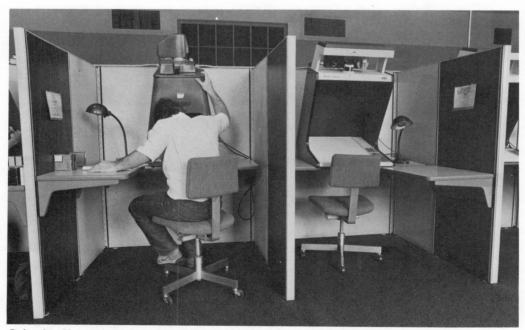

Columbia University solution to the problem of note-taking while using microfilm.

Some institutions have spent a great deal of money to develop customized carrels which can be adjusted so that the reader can have the machine at the height and

angle best for him/her. Interviews conducted with
staff and patrons at one such library revealed that the
adjustments are seldom made. A much less expensive
solution is the use of secretarial chairs with posture
adjustment for both height and angle. The authors have
also found that a small strip of wood can be inserted
under the front or rear of a machine to change the
angle just a few degrees for a patron who is
uncomfortable.

Strips of plug-mold can be fastened to the
underside of the carrels or tables to carry electrical
power to the machines. The plug-mold can be fed from
below the floor, from building columns, or from the
ceiling above by suspending some attractive chrome
tubes.

Printing Area:

Regular reader-printers can be dispersed throughout
the reading area or grouped together. If a machine is
to be used solely for printing it should be placed near
the service desk where the activity around the machine
will be less distracting to patrons in the reading
area. The print-only machines might well be coin-
operated. A change machine might be provided in a very
active microform area. We have found it advisable to
place print-only machines on standing height tables and
provide no chairs. The space per machine should still
be planned at 40 square feet, however, because there
may be someone waiting in addition to the user of the

machine. If the library is using regular reader-
printers for printing only, they will be quite slow.
Under those circumstances a tall stool should be
available for the use of patrons with extensive
copying. Ideally a production speed machine should be
available because the only thing more frustrating than
using a slow machine to make a large number of copies
is waiting for someone who is making a large number of
copies.

Storage Area:

   If the storage area is to be closed to the public
it should be placed behind the service desk. It should
be as square as possible to avoid staff having to
travel the entire length of a rectangular space. It
should be arranged so that the most frequently used
materials are nearest the service area.

   If the storage area is to be open to the public, it
should be set up so that one can move from the reading
area to the adjacent storage area without passing a
large number of other reading positions. In other
words, two parallel rectangular areas of reading and
storage should be planned so that one need never pass
through more than the width of the reading area.

   The storage area should have the same minimum floor
loading as a conventional bookstack (150 pounds per
square foot) and should be planned for substantial
expansion and with a view toward avoiding the future
shifting of storage cabinets or stacks. A fully loaded

High storage density, but difficult access—typical in many libraries.

floor model storage cabinet with a companion unit on
top of it weighs approximately 1,100 pounds. Emptying,
shifting, and refilling cabinets is costly and time

consuming. If a closed area is definitely to remain closed somewhat narrower aisles can be used than in an open access collection, but if there is any chance that the storage area will be opened to the patrons--and the trend is definitely in that direction--it is wise to plan the wider public aisles.

In some libraries the microform master copies are also shelved in the microform area. These are the originals from which the service or reference copies have been made. In most libraries the masters would be of local newspapers or archival materials. We recommend against storing these in the same location as the service copies because everything could be destroyed in a fire or flood. It also may result in staff using a master copy periodically when the service copy is not available.

Staff area:

The staff must be accommodated near the entrance to the area. Staff should be highly visible to persons walking into the area. The service desk should control the storage area in a closed stacks collection and yet it should have good visual control of the reading area, not just to protect materials and machines, but also to identify patrons who may need assistance. The catalog of the collection should also be placed near the entry for the public and for easy access by the staff.

If there is a desk rather than a counter,

additional storage should be provided for portable
microform readers, paper for the reader-printers, and
other supplies which will be needed in the reading
area. A work room is absolutely essential. There must
be a place for inspecting, cleaning, and repairing
microform. Repair of microform is not a simple
operation. It requires special equipment, materials
and skills. It cannot be properly done by an attendant
sitting at a public service desk.

Equipment in the work room should include a film
inspection and splicing desk with a light box for
examining microform, a rewinder for roll film, and a
splicing machine. Some storage space for microform
being handled should be provided. There should also be
storage space for microform supplies, including basic
spare parts for the machines. If a film cleaner is
owned, it might be housed here.

Display Area:

Bulletin boards and display cases are an excellent
way to call attention to little used materials which
are potentially valuable or to new materials the
library has acquired.

Special Touches:

Well-planned graphics both to direct patrons to the
microform area and to identify the various materials
and machine types are not only informative, but can

also add to patron comfort in using the microform
facility.

Pennsylvania State University Library microform publicity.

One major microform facility was enhanced by the
addition of attractive framed prints and posters on the
walls and hanging plants near the windows. The area
has a warmth that is uncommon in microform facilities
in most other libraries. A budget of less than $150
was required to provide these special touches.

University of Michigan Library promotion for ERIC microfiche.

Imaginative display at the University of Massachusetts.

Example of a typical unattractive reading area which has since been remodeled.

Prints and plants in a microform area.

IV
Selection and Maintenance
of
Equipment

SELECTION AND MAINTENANCE
OF EQUIPMENT

Microform equipment should be selected with both
suitability for the user and maintenance in mind.
Selection of good equipment will promote user
satisfaction initially, but only good maintenance
will lead to long-term user satisfaction. Observers
such as Francis Spreitzer have commented again and
again that the basic problem with equipment in use in
libraries comes not from its age or design, but from
its condition, which tends to be poor.

In addition to discussing equipment used by
library patrons, it is necessary to describe filming
and processing equipment because a few libraries may
want to do their own microfilming. Normally, in-house
filming is not undertaken to conserve space because the
cost of producing a single microform copy of a printed
work would wipe out the value of any space savings
realized. Only commercial and cooperative filming
programs normally produce enough copies over which to
spread the initial filming costs to make microform an
economically attractive medium. Libraries usually
undertake filming in-house because there are
local newspapers which are not being filmed elsewhere,
local archives require protection, or unique special
collections are thought to warrant preservation.

Microform Cameras:

A microform camera films original documents and produces microfilm or microfiche. The basic camera types are rotary, planetary, and step-and-repeat. The rotary camera is generally the least expensive and the fastest, systematically filming an average of 250 correspondence size loose pages per minute, with some expensive units capable of three times that throughput.

The originals or documents as they are normally called by the vendors of the equipment (each page is a "document") must be of uniform size and thickness and free of staples or paperclips. Documents are fed in on a moving belt either manually or automatically. The rotary camera requires cutting up books or journals into separate sheets. The front and back of a sheet of paper may be filmed simultaneously and the sheet may be of any length. Reductions normally range from 13X to 45X. Most of the equipment now on the market produces 16mm film.

With a planetary camera, the original and the film remain motionless during exposure. The original document remains on a level plane surface at the time of filming and the camera is suspended overhead. The camera can be moved up and down to change the reduction ratio. Only one side of a document can be filmed at a time. Since there is considerable distance between the camera and the surface of the table, it is possible to film bound journals and books without cutting them up.

Most planetary cameras are 35mm and are, therefore, suitable for filming newspapers. The stationary image, the width of the film, and several other factors provide a better resolution than with the rotary camera.

Step-and-repeat cameras, many of which look like planetary cameras, expose a series of images on a sheet of film in multiple rows. The camera does the positioning automatically. Most cameras of this type use 105mm film because the end product is usually microfiche. This is the most costly type of camera, often over $30,000; but it avoids the labor of producing fiche by jacketing 16mm microfilm and it has a throughput substantially greater than the planetary camera. Some models can accept bound books and journals, thus increasing the flexibility of the equipment.

The selection of camera equipment should be made only after a careful analysis of the work to be done and of the options available. The fact that almost all libraries have invested in planetary cameras does not mean that this is the best choice for all libraries. Much in-house microfilming by libraries has been of newpapers, usually local and esoteric foreign titles. For newspaper filming the planetary camera is an excellent choice. A rotary camera would be a good choice for filming large archival collections because it is very fast. A rotary camera should not be used for fragile materials or very thin paper, however. The

3M Step-and-Repeat Camera (Courtesy: 3M Company).

step-and-repeat is an excellent choice for annual reports, journals and government documents because it combines the benefits of the rotary's speed and the planetary's flexibility. The fiche which are normally produced with the step-and-repeat camera are easy to file, retrieve, and duplicate.

Among the things to look for in selecting any camera are the ease of loading the film, ease of operation of the control panel, the availability of automatic exposure control, and the throughput. The first two of these are self explanatory. Automatic exposure control requires some discussion. Constant line density, the most essential requirement for good subsequent reproduction, is best assured by an automatic exposure control system. A good operator may be able to make manual adjustments using a camera without this feature, but the rate of filming will be reduced. The automatic exposure control constantly and rapidly checks not only the contrast of the document being filmed but also the incident light in the environment in which the filming is being done. Constant adjustment in the length of the exposure then assures easier reading and better reproductions later.

Selecting a machine which is too slow or fast for the amount of work to be done is the most common error we have encountered. An effective way to choose among machines with different rates of speed is to add the machine's one time cost, the cost of supplies over a five year period, and the cost of labor over a five

year period. The lowest total five-year cost is
normally what one should seek. A slow machine may cost
a great deal more in labor cost over five years. Too
fast a machine may cut labor costs, but the higher
initial purchase price may make it unattractive.

As with any equipment, ease of maintenance is an
important factor. We recommend that insofar as
possible the library limit consideration to equipment
for which there is local maintenance available.

Train operators carefully, even on the most simple
equipment. Even with simple controls and warning lamps
or buzzers, inexperienced operators can load film
improperly, continue filming after the film is used up,
or make any number of other mistakes. If a library is
not able or willing to hire or develop qualified
people, a service bureau is a better way to get filming
done. Again there is a rule of thumb: filming is
usually done more cost-effectively and with more
consistent quality by a service bureau if the annual
filming volume is less than 250,000 pages per year.

While this book emphasizes the facilities aspect
of microform, it is necessary to remind ourselves that
the filming of material does not begin with the
pressing of the button on the camera. There is
considerable preparation required of that which is to
be filmed. Decisions have to be made about what to
film, using what microformat and emulsion, the
reduction ratio must be decided, and the decision made

whether to retain or discard the material after filming. Eye-legible bibliographic and information targets have to be made for inclusion in the filming.

A visit to the Library of Congress, the New York Public Library, or the MIT Library is a must for anyone contemplating a large-scale microfilming program using more than one camera. For those who plan only a single unit, the specifications and standard practices instructions which these libraries have prepared for their staffs are invaluable.

Processing:

After film has been exposed it must be developed, fixed, washed, and dried. These steps are usually performed inside an automatic processor. These processors are normally classified by film width. In moderate volume filming operations the functions of filming and processing are combined in a single unit called a processor-camera. A library which has a microfilm camera(s) has the option of acquiring its own processor(s) or using a commercial processing service. Should a library decide to do its own processing, it should normally get a unit which requires no special plumbing facilities or darkroom. The newer model low to moderate volume processors only require periodic replacement of water and chemicals rather than a constant supply. The water can be obtained by running a hose from any nearby sink or other water source. The extra cost of special plumbing is warranted only if extremely large volumes of film are to be processed.

Darkrooms too are not necessary in most cases because processing is done inside the equipment.

Inspection Equipment:

Processed film may be inspected at an inspection station or a table with a lightbox over which the microform is passed for viewing. Some commercially available inspection tables come with magnifying lenses while others project the image onto a screen. Various optional features include a densitometer for measuring the opacity of the film and a microscope for measuring resolution. Many units also include a splicer. It is possible to spend as much as $5,000 on an inspection station, but many libraries spend less than half that by purchasing each of the components separately.

Splicers:

Every library with microfilm should have a splicer. Torn film should never be mended with ordinary cellophane tape. There is special archival-quality transparent tape available for emergency repairs in the reading area, but permanent repairs should be made as soon as possible using a heat or cement splicer. The former, also known as a butt-weld splicer because one butts rather than overlaps the film when splicing, costs approximately $700 and does a fast and permanent job. The latter often costs less than $100 and is somewhat slower.

Newspaper film splicer.

Splices done with cement are overlapping. They should be allowed to set overnight before returning the microfilm to the collection.

Microfiche is less frequently damaged, but it can normally also be spliced. An alternative for badly damaged microfiche is to replace it. A fiche-to-fiche copy can be made on the library's own equipment or the publisher will do so, sometimes for as little as $.75.

Reading Equipment:

A microform reader is used to provide the microfilmed information in a readily visible form. A variety of readers is available. The choice will depend on need. Basic types include:

1. <u>Lap readers</u>. Designed for compactness. Only available as fiche readers. The smallest of these is a hand-held viewer priced at less than $80. The optics are satisfactory for field use, but the authors recommend the purchase of portable readers if a library wishes to make readers available on loan.

Folding hand viewer for fiche.

2. <u>Portable readers</u>. Designed to be carried in a small suitcase. The weight is usually less than 15 pounds. Some have batteries. A wide variety of fiche readers and a few film readers are now available. Some of the fiche readers are extremely durable and offer excellent quality images. The best choice for libraries is one of the models with a rotating turret mechanism because it provides maximum security for up to three lenses.

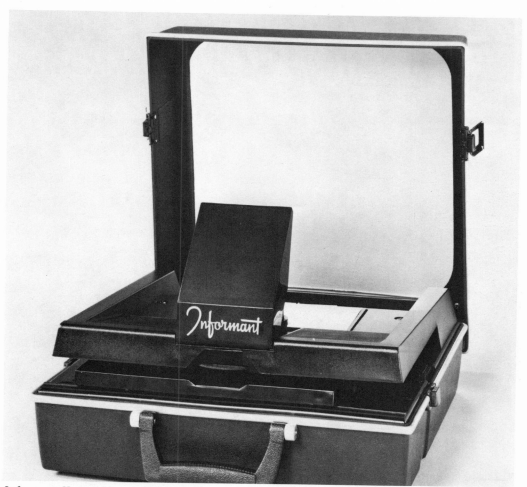

Informant II portable microfiche reader.

3. <u>Desk readers</u>. Designed for use on a desk or
    table. The most common in libraries. It is
    extremely important that suitable tables and
    carrells be purchased to accompany the units.

Two types of desk readers in use at Dartmouth University.

4. Free-standing units. Once very common (the
    Recordak Model C, for example), but now less
    so. Manufacturers have sought to hold the
    price of equipment down so they have elimin-
    ated bases or cabinets. They also argue that
    desk readers provide the purchaser with
    more flexibility.

The discussion which follows assumes that the
library will normally procure desk readers for most of
the reading positions in the library. The suggestions
for determining quantities apply only to units to be
kept in the library. There are too few libraries
lending portable equipment to provide formulae for
estimating quantities. While the discussion of
features to look for in readers are aimed primarily at
desk readers, they can be judiciously applied to other
types.

Number of Readers Required:

The number of microform readers available should be
adequate to provide for periods of peak demand for each
type of microform held by a library. While that is
normally learned by observation, there is a rule of
thumb for estimating the requirement in a library that
has as many microform pieces as it has bound volumes:
one piece of reading equipment for each 200 persons who
enter the building in the course of a day. The rule of
thumb is based on observations at several institutions.
The number of people coming to the library is more

important than the number of microform holdings in
determining the number of reading machines once a
substantial (normally a volume equivalent of 10% or
more of the hard-copy collection) microform collection
has been established.

Many libraries determine the distribution of
readers on the basis of holdings by format. If half
the holdings are in fiche, half the readers would then
be microfiche readers. That often works, but if the
roll film collection includes the New York Times, a
local newspaper and several popular journals, the fact
that the film collection is small won't matter very
much. It is more appropriate to look at the use
statistics for each format for the previous year. If
one's collection is brand new, comparison with a
similar microform collection elsewhere would be a
solution. If one is unable to make any kind of
estimate, purchase units half and half using up to 80%
of one's reading machine budget and hold the rest of
the funds in reserve pending some experience with user
demand. We strongly recommend against investing in
multi-purpose machines which allegedly read all
microform formats because they often confuse many users
and often require more service calls.

Keep in mind that while a good roll film reader
costs from $1,000 to $3,000, an excellent microfiche
reader can be purchased for $250 to $400. It is,
therefore, easier to adjust the number of fiche readers
after the initial equipment installation has been made.

Dukane microfilm and microfiche reader.

Failure to provide an adequate number of readers
is even more serious than failing to provide an
adequate number of regular reading positions in a
library unless the library circulates its microforms.

Selecting Readers:

There are several factors to be considered in
selecting reading equipment. The most important are:

1. Ease of use:
The machine must be so straightforward that even
the first-time user who approaches it without the
assistance of a library staff member will be able to
use it with minimum trial and error. All controls
should be clearly visible and graphics should
illustrate their use. Microfilm readers should include
a threading diagram. A patron should never have to
remove or install lenses. It should be possible to
scan with one hand. Ideally the scanner control will
be on the front of the machine to facilitate use by
either right or left handed persons. This also permits
taking notes with the free hand.

It should be possible to move film forward and
backward smoothly and at various speeds. Manual
machines should have both fast and slow speed cranks
and motorized units should have the ability to adjust
the speed from very fast to very slow. Inability to
scan very slowly without a jerking, blurring motion of
the image is often a problem with motorized units.

Microfiche reader considerations are similar, but the specific questions to be asked include the constancy of the frame-to-frame focus and the ease of the frame-to-frame scanning capability.

It should be possible to rotate the image at least 180 degrees in a rollfilm reader and 90 degrees in a fiche reader so that material filmed at an angle can be comfortably read.

2. Image quality:

There should be a sharp image across the width of the screen. There must be no shadowy fringes along the edges of the text, nor may there be "hot spots" or bright areas near the center. The lamp should remain at the same intensity during its life. The image should stay in focus when the frame is changed. It should be possible to increase or decrease the light intensity. An opaque screen should be hooded to limit ambient light falling on the screen. The screen should be made of non-glare materials and should be scratch resistant.

The screen size, color, magnification, and quality of the optical system will not only affect the ease and comfort of reading the material, but also the attitude of the user.

3. Adaptability:

A microfilm reader should accommodate both 16mm

and 35mm film unless the library is firmly wedded to
only one film size. Ideally, it should have more than
one lens to permit one to enlarge the images once the
required text is identified. It should be possible to
rotate the images at least 180 degrees. The screen
should be at least 11 inches high to permit reading of
a full manuscript page if that is the primary
application. It should be at least 22 inches high if
many newspapers are to be read.

A microfiche reader should have built-in dual
lenses so that fiche of both 24X and 42X or 48X can be
read in the same machine. It should not be necessary
to remove one lens from the machine in order to use the
other. A micro-opaque reader should ideally
accommodate both microprint and the nearly defunct
Microcard ® .

All equipment should be capable of being plugged
into conventional electrical outlets.

   4. Noise level:

It should be possible to operate equipment in
reading areas committed to serious, quiet study. Not
only must the noise level of a cooling fan be low, but
the machine should produce no sharp noises as parts are
moved. Listen carefully to the machine in a show room,
but preferably observe it in a library environment
before making a commitment to purchase.

Realist Vantage III microform reader with lenses which must be removed to be changed.

5. Protection of microform:

Microform loading should be simple so damage is minimized. Pressure plates should lift up when microform is being loaded or advanced so that the microform will not be scratched. In fiche readers one

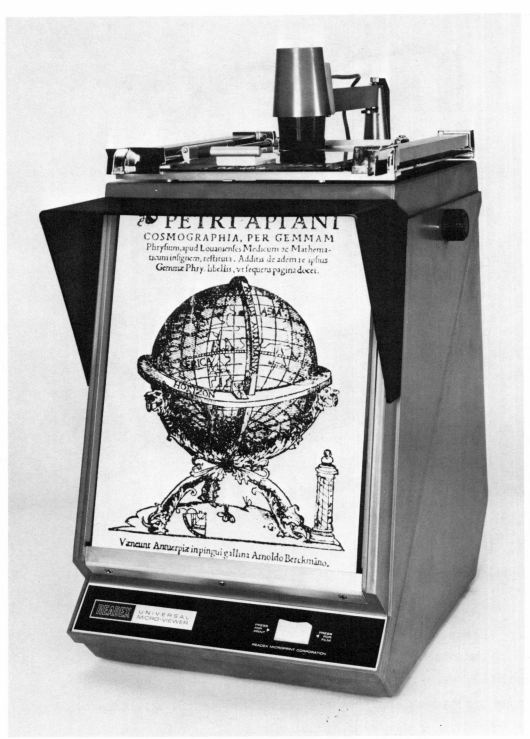

*Readex Universal Micro-Viewer for both opaque and transparent microform
(Courtesy: Readex Microprint Corporation).*

Readex Opaque Viewer microform reader (Courtesy: Readex Microprint Corporation).

should check on the self-opening flats for changing
fiche to make sure the fiche are protected from direct
contact with the lens. The microform should not be
damaged if it is left unattended in the machine for up
to an hour (microform is damaged when its temperature
is raised above 167 degrees F).

6. <u>Durability</u>:

The general construction of the machine should be
rugged. There should be no parts protruding from the
machine that can be easily knocked off. All knobs
should be secured with screws or threads. There should
be no dangling parts which can be damaged (e.g., the
transport control at the end of a power cable on some
readers). The machine should not get so hot that bulbs
burn out quickly or that microform is damaged. A
motorized unit should have a heavy-duty motor that is
capable of driving the transport at various speeds and
able to handle frequent reversals in direction. A
library should be very sure that it needs motorized
units because the motorized transport mechanisms are
usually the greatest source of machine malfunction in
the facilities we have visited.

7. <u>Maintenance</u>:

The reader should be easy to clean so preventive
maintenance of lenses, pressure plates, and screens can
be done regularly. The lenses and pressure plates
should, nevertheless, be well protected from dust. The
screen should be shatterproof and be easy to replace.
The light bulb should be a long-life bulb so that
changes need be made only infrequently. It must be
possible to change the light bulb quickly and safely.
One of the authors remembers being the only member of
the staff in a library of 75 full-time staff who would
change the bulbs on a particular model of microfilm

reader because the bulbs regularly broke of their sockets when one attempted to unscrew them. A large number of readers were always "out-of-order" simply because the bulbs had burned out.

Local repair service should be available, if not from the manufacturer, at least from another source. A spare parts inventory should be retained somewhere in or near the community, including not only frequently replaced parts such as bulbs, but also those which are seldom replaced. A library cannot afford to wait a week or more for parts which have to be ordered from the manufacturer.

8. Cost:

Purchase price is important, but the lowest price may not be a bargain if bulbs are very expensive (they range from $.75 to more than $35.00) and must be changed frequently. A low price is also no bargain if repairs are expensive or must be made more frequently than with machines which cost more initially. A special low price may mean that a machine is about to be discontinued. A manufacturer should be prepared to represent that it plans to continue production of the machine for at least three more years.

9. Manufacturer's Reputation:

Does the manufacturer have an established reputation for producing a quality product? Does it have regular representation in or near the library's community? It has been said that one buys not just a product, one "buys a company."

Other Considerations:

The screen is the surface onto which the image is projected. Front projection units and rear projection units of comparable quality are now being manufactured. The former projects the image onto an opaque screen using reflected light; the latter projects it through a translucent screen from inside the reader for viewing from the opposite side. The front projection units using the opaque screen must either be viewed in a room with subdued lighting or the machines must be equipped with a hood to keep light from the windows or the light fixtures from reflecting off the screen. If light control is a problem, this type of unit should be avoided. An advantage of many front projection units is that the screen is flush with the reading table only a few inches above the table. Rear projection units usually have screens which are vertical to the table. This requires some adjustment in note taking because most people are accustomed to taking notes from a horizontal original. Vertical screens are also uncomfortable for wearers of bifocals because of the constant need to change focus.

Translucent screens must be tinted to avoid eye fatique from too much light passing through them. This may distort color in color microform. The authors,

Micro Design 935 front projection microfiche reader.

Micro Design rear projection fiche reader model 955.

therefore, recommend front projection units for use with color microform.

Keep the number of makes and models of machines to a minimum. That does not mean a single one, but it does mean avoiding the purchase of different machines each year because of changing prices. It also means exercising great caution in accepting "free" machines as premiums with the purchase of microforms. Patrons get confused when what they learn in using a machine one day cannot be applied to another machine for the same microformat a day later. Even good instructions on the machine aren't enough to offset the frustration of being compelled to learn again and again.

A library should purchase covers with the viewing equipment to protect the units against dust. The covers can be removed from as many machines as are expected to be used in a day. Rather than purchasing the dull covers supplied by vendors, a library might make its own covers out of colorful fabrics to enliven the reading area.

Each machine should be purchased with one or more copies of an owner's manual and at least a one-year supply of spare bulbs.

National Archives Evaluation:

While it is not the purpose of this book to recommend specific pieces of equipment, it is appropriate to call attention to the results of one of the most extensive user evaluations of microfilm readers ever conducted. It was undertaken by the National Archives and Records Service in 1973. Several of the eight machines used in the survey are still available, among them is the top-rated machine, the

ID 201 Reader (Courtesy: University of Michigan).

I.D. 201, a product of Information Design, Inc. Of the eighty users who tried at least four machines, this unit was rated best for film loading and unloading, film winding and unwinding, focusing, scanning, image rotation, location of controls, size of screen, and screen illumination. Over 68% rated the machine as higly satisfactory, 28% as satisfactory, and less than 4% unsatisfactory. Nearly 57% rated it the best of the eight machines in the study. Of those who had used a reader less than 10 times, a common thing in most libraries, over 64% rated it best.

This desk top model reader accommodates both 16 and 35mm rollfilm. It is available in manual and motorized models, but the manual is far more reliable. The screen size is a generous 24 by 24 inches. The magnification is 18X. This makes the unit less attractive than one which has multiple lenses, which would allow one to blow up an image.

The Library Microforms and Materials Company (LMM) is the only other company which is still producing a roll film reader which had high ratings in the survey. It is a stand-alone unit and is somewhat more expensive than the I.D. 201, primarily because it comes in a handsome carrel.

There are other good machines available that should also be considered.

The LMM microfilm reader has its own carrel (Courtesy: Michigan State University).

Reader-Printers and Printers:

The ability to print paper copies from the microform collection is imperative because patrons must be able to avoid the taking of notes by hand in the same way they are able to avoid laborious copying with printed books and journals. A library should be able to produce prints from any of the microform formats it has chosen to include in its collection.

The factors enumerated for the selection of reading equipment also apply to the selection of printing equipment:

    1. Ease of use
    2. Image quality
    3. Adaptability

4. Low noise level
5. Protection of microform
6. Durability
7. Maintenance
8. Cost

It is sometimes argued that ease of use is less important because many libraries make the copies for their users. There is a growing trend toward self-service, however, and high staff turnover, especially among student assistants in academic libraries, makes it desirable to have straigthfoward equipment in almost every library.

When evaluating the printer component of a reader-printer, it is particularly important to determine that the copy corresponds to the images seen on the screen. It should reproduce all of the text and it should do so with the same clarity and contrast as the screen image. It is likely that a machine which projects an unsatisfactory image on the screen will also make unsatisfactory copies. It does not follow that a good screen image will result in good hard copies.

Many users make only a few copies so it is important that the first copy produced be satisfactory or the wastage will be high. Both image quality and ease of alignment are important in this regard.

If it is important that all prints produced be positive (black on white) and if the library has both negative and positive microform, it is important that

The 3M reader-printer, one of the most widely used in libraries.

Minolta RP 405 reader-printer, a current best seller (Courtesy: University Microfilms International).

the capacity to do both with a simple adjustment be
clearly established at the time the machine is selected.

Some reader-printers are annoying to use because they are noisy and there are flashes of light during the printing process. Also some equipment have poor

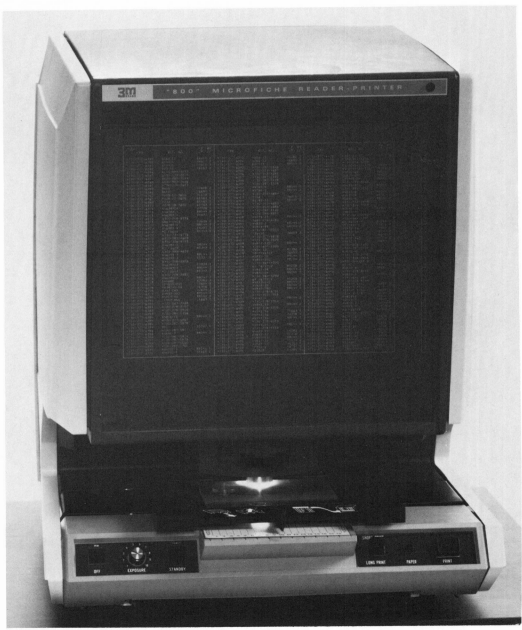

3M Model "800" Microfiche Reader-Printer.

paper transport mechanisms or use messy chemicals which give off strong odors and gum up the machine parts. These negative characteristics are common to many of the older machines currently in use in libraries and to some of the inexpensive models now on the market.

A library should not only use a check list such as the following when purchasing new printing equipment, but should also use it to evaluate existing equipment periodically. Unsatisfactory printing equipment can make a million-dollar microform collection unattractive to potential users. The checklist which follows is adapted from one used by Library Technology Reports:

1. Prints should be of high quality, whether positive or negative microform is used.
2. Copies should correspond to the screen images.
3. The equipment should be easy to use.
4. First copies printed should be usable.
5. The copies should be dry to the touch.
6. It should be possible to write on the copies.
7. Copies should be long-lasting.
8. The cost-per-copy should average $.05 or less.
9. Microform should not be damaged.
10. There should be very little downtime.

LTR has used these criteria in evaluating large numbers of reader-printers. They make over 1,000 prints per machine in a single month using a variety of microform, including special test microform. The details of the testing procedure are given in a special Council on Library Resources publication by William R. Hawken entitled Evaluating Microfiche Readers.[15]

---

[15]Hawken, William R. Evaluating Microfiche Readers, Washington: Council on Library Resources, 1975.

There appears to be one thing overlooked in LTR's
careful testing. They do not use a machine only
occasionally with long periods between copies and a
lack of preventive maintenance. Some machines
withstand this type of environment, which is common in
libraries, much better than others. Contacts with
libraries similar to one's own which have the type of
equipment one is considering is absolutely essential
for this reason.

Ideally a library would have printing capability
at all reading positions, but that costs more than most
libraries can afford. A few college and special
libraries have as many as 50% of the reading positions
equipped with reader-printers. An absolute minimum
appears to be one reader-printer for each ten reading
machines.

If a library can afford only one or two
reader-printers, it should be careful to select a unit
which adapts easily from one format to another. A
number of libraries have reader-printers which require
a difficult 5 minute installation process to change
from negative to positive or from microfiche to
microfilm. Most machines which do one or two things
well cannot do everything well. For that reason two
machines, one each for microfilm and microfiche, are
far better than one.

Plain paper reader-printers were still uncommon in
libraries in 1980. There were only two machines of

this type in general use. Most of the equipment used
either the electrostatic or "Dry Silver"® process. The
first requires a liquid toner and the latter a
specially coated paper. The latter is up to twice as
expensive per copy due to recent dramatic increases in
the cost of the materials used. The former should be
adopted only if the library will keep the machines in
extremely good working order because quality
deteriorates rapidly when machine care slips.

Most libraries charge for copies made on
reader-printers. Fees range dramatically, from $.05 to

A positive dry-silver print from a negative screen image on the 3M 500 Reader-Printer.

$1.00 per copy, but $.10 appears to be the most
common. The library should consider attaching a coinbox to at least some of the machines to avoid constant
collection of small amounts of money. The equipment
vendor can normally be given the responsibility for
supplying and installing the coinbox. It should be one
which can be reset because prices are likely to change
within the life of the equipment.

Production Copying:

The making of a copy of an entire monograph,
government document, or extensive article on a
reader-printer is laborious and frustrating. More and
more libraries are installing machines which are
designed to be used for printing only. The screen
tends to be smaller and the throughput much faster.
Some units (the Xerox 970 Microfiche Printing System
for example) are capable of producing as many as 3300
copies per hour on plain bond paper. A large system of
this type leases for several hundred dollars per month,
but the per copy cost is well under $.05.

There are production machines available for as
little as $200 per month rental or a purchase price of
less than $10,000. At first it may seem a great deal
of money to spend, but when one compares this
investment in equipment to make the microform
collection more usable with the much larger amount the
library has already invested in equipment to make
copies from printed materials or in the microform
collection itself, the figure appears reasonable.

Duplicating Equipment:

In most libraries, providing good service also means offering microform copies of library-owned microforms so that patrons may take copies for use on their own equipment.

Roll film duplicating equipment is available, but most libraries will not find it cost effective to own because the equipment is geared to high production applications and entire reels of film are only infrequently duplicated in most libraries. When only a few frames are needed, the use of a reader-printer is better.

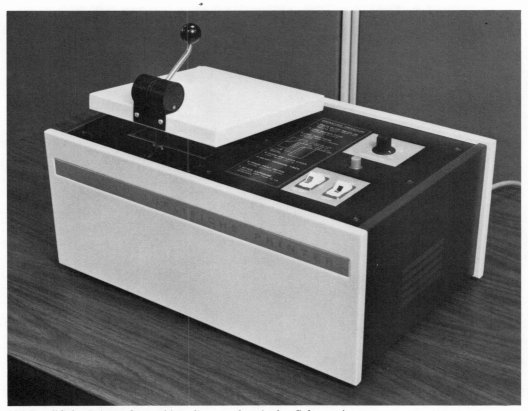

3M Duplifiche Printer for making diazo and vesicular fiche copies.

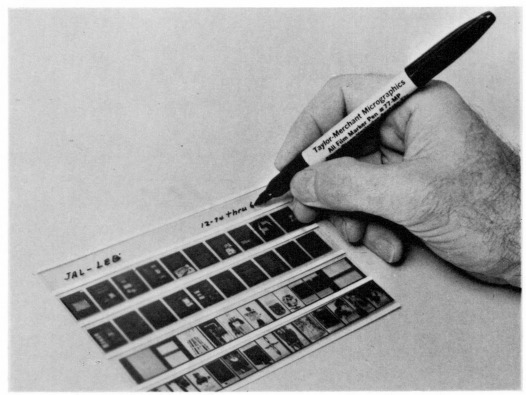

Taylor-Merchant Micrographics pen for marking headers on duplicated fiche.

Fiche-to-fiche duplication is another matter. Low cost duplicating equipment is available. A $2,200 unit can make up to 150 duplicates per hour at a cost of as little as $.06 per fiche produced, exclusive of labor. Higher speed units are available with 750 to 1,500 fiche per hour production capabilities.

Film Cleaning Machines:

Roll film must periodically be cleaned by running it through a special cleaning machine. Dust, dirt, fingerprints and other substances on the film can be

Kineclean microfilm cleaning machine.

removed quickly and safely. The machines to do this
range from chemical units costing just over $1,000 to
ultrasonic units costing well over $10,000. The less
expensive chemical equipment is suitable for most
libraries. It will clean a 100 foot reel of film in
just under 3 minutes. Three gallons of cleaning
solution, a year's supply for most libraries, costs
less than $100. The same solution can be used to wipe
microfiche. Gloves should be worn while using
chemicals and all work should be done in a well
ventilated area.

A library might clean its most heavily used microform once a year and the rest once in three or more years. The cleaning cycle should be set by observing local conditions--use, cleanliness of the storage area, etc.

Equipment Maintenance:

Equipment care is more than replacing bulbs or repairing malfunctioning parts. Equipment can seriously damage microform while apparently operating normally. In order to protect microform a library should clean all parts of the reader in contact with the film using clean, soft, lint-free cloth at least once a week, preferably daily. Screens and mirrors should be cleaned and the rollers should be inspected for rough spots that might scratch the microform whenever the cleaning is being done. It is a good idea to use a short strip of clear microform in each machine to check for scratching. Inserting and removing, winding and rewinding, and otherwise simulating normal use will reveal any tendency of the equipment to scratch the microform.

Simple repairs can often be done by library staff. More complex repairs should be done by a professional service specialist. While maintenance agreements are often not an economically sound investment, establishing an agreement for remedial service as needed is. It should take no more than a telephone call to get a service specialist. No

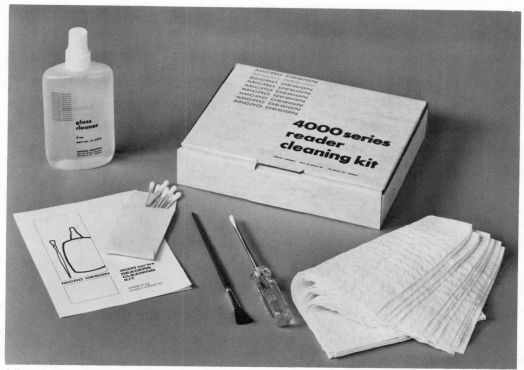

Micro Design microform reader cleaning kit.

purchase orders should be necessary and no review of qualifications and negotiation of rates. Those things should be taken care of once at the beginning of each year.

A machine service record should be kept on each unit so that it wil be possible to determine when a machine is not being properly repaired or when it has such a variety of problems that it is not worth retaining. A simple 3 by 5 inch card or other form for each machine is usually sufficient. The problem, the date, and the person completing the repairs should be noted.

Sources of Information About Equipment:

The most comprehensive overview of microform
equipment is the National Micrographics Association
publication entitled Guide to Microreproduction
Equipment and its supplements. It is available by mail
from the Association's headquarters in Silver Spring,
MD. Reviews of specific pieces of equipment of
interest to libraries can be obtained from
Micrographics Equipment Review, an annual publication
sponsored by Microform Review Inc. (priced at $100 to
$150 per year) and from Library Technology Reports
($150 per year for 6 issues). The former attempts to
provide librarians with information about approximately
80% of the new pieces of equipment which become
available each year. The latter does periodic
overviews of all significant equipment on the market at
that time. For example, the March-April, 1979 issue of
Library Technology Reports devoted approximately 200
pages to reader-printers and the July-August, 1979
issue had an equally long article on microform storage
equipment and supplies.

New Library World of Great Britain also has annual
review articles on new equipment that are much broader
in coverage than Micrographics Equipment Review, but
with somewhat less information about each piece of
equipment.

The majority of the librarians with whom the
authors have talked keep informed through frequent
contacts with experts in the field. The informal

exchange of information and views appears to influence actual decisions more than published sources. While the authors share the opinion that contacts with experts is the best source of current information, they are concerned that most librarians talk only with other librarians. It has been their experience that experts in business and industry can be an excellent source of information about equipment and procedures because it is in those fields that microform is most regularly used. It is an excellent idea for a librarian to attend one or more trade shows aimed at commercial microform users to look at equipment and to hear other points of view.

Demonstrations and trial periods remain the best way for a librarian to acquire invaluable first-hand experience with a variety of equipment. One must sometimes be insistent with a salesperson to do this, but it is worth the temporary discomfort.

V
Storage Equipment

STORAGE EQUIPMENT

Microform should normally be stored in closed
containers so as to protect them from dirt and
atmospheric pollution. Roll film should be kept wound,
not too tightly, on reels. The reels should be kept in
boxes of stainless steel, aluminum, peroxide-free
plastic, or non-acidic cardboard. Fiche should be kept
in individual acid-free paper envelopes or other acid-
free holders. These individual storage media can then
be filed in any one of a number of different types of
storage units. Libraries normally use only conventional book shelving and microform storage cabinets,
but business and industry use a much wider range. Some
of the storage devices now infrequently used by
libraries should be considered by them, especially for
microform which are in heavy demand or which need to be
promoted.

Factors in Selection:

There are a number of factors which should be
weighed before selecting storage equipment. There is
no perfect storage medium which is suitable for all
situations. Several will be discussed here:

    Formats--Each of the formats described in Chapter
    Two may, depending on the quantity and type of
    use, require a different type of storage. Even
    when a library interfiles all materials in the
    collection, as Central State University of

Oklahoma and Guelph University of Ontario do,
there are still options for putting material in
special storage containers before putting them on
the book shelves.

Size of Collection--The number of items and the
rate of new acquisition should greatly influence
the storage system chosen. For example, a fiche
collection which consists of only the most
current telephone directories for major metro-
politan areas can easily be stored in two plastic
trays, while an on-going subscription to all of
the ERIC documents on requires a storage system
which can accommodate several hundred thousand
fiche.

Use of the Materials--The pattern of use of the
collections should play an important role in
determining the appropriate storage system. A
little used collection can be stored in low-cost
units, a collection of master copies can and
should be stored in very secure storage equipment, and an actively used collection should be
housed in durable and easily used equipment. A
small collection which is frequently used might
be housed in fiche panels attached to the reader
rather than stored in a cabinet several feet
away.

Open or Closed Stacks--The type of storage
selected depends in part on the degree of public

access provided. The first several types described in this chapter are most suitable for materials which are frequently accessed by the library's patrons. Storage cabinets are suitable for public access if well marked. They are also an effective storage medium for closed stacks. Bookstacks are suitable for access by the general public only if the microform are shelved one-deep. The use of storage boxes on the shelves or filing two-deep is suitable only in limited access storage areas because it takes more time to find and retrieve materials.

Location of Materials--If the microform is to be stored in a public area some attention should be paid to the color and finish of the storage equipment. Durability is also important when a wide variety of users will get the microform from the equipment. Equipment in closed storage areas might be selected for economy and storage efficiency rather than appearance or outstanding durability.

Security of Collections--If security is a concern, storage cabinets with locks should be purchased. Metal bars with padlocks can be purchased for the locking of cabinets which were purchased without locks, but they are a nuisance to use. It is also possible to purchase some storage units on casters so that they can be moved into a locked area when the staff cannot look after them.

<u>Potential Damage</u>--Areas which are near a radiator or which have sunny windows which cannot be covered should not have open storage or uninsulated storage. Materials should not be stored within 3 inches of the floor in areas underneath water pipes or below ground level.

<u>Space Available</u>--The accurate measurement of dimensions, including height, is important in calculating the amount of aisle space needed for the full extension of drawers, for using space below windows effectively, etc.

<u>Available Funds</u>--Libraries must sometimes purchase that which fits within the budget, rather than that which is most suitable. Under such circumstances it should still be possible to apply the most important of the other criteria.

The storage equipment chosen should reflect all of the aforementioned criteria to as great an extent as the situation permits. The authors feel that regardless of the format, the type of users, or location, ease of use should be considered as an overriding consideration. The attitudes of library staff and patrons will determine the success of the microform program. The selection of storage equipment that is highly cost effective or secure, but unpopular with users is counterproductive.

The most common types of storage which are available will be described in the following sections. Information about specific products is available from several sources. The July/August, 1979 issue of Library Technology Reports contains an extensive survey of the microform storage products most commonly used by libraries. Almost all of the products mentioned are currently being marketed. The issue also has a list of U. S. vendors. IRM: Information and Records Management, a monthly journal, is the best source for storage products most commonly purchased by business and industry.

Fiche Storage:

Binders are a convenient way of storing fiche. Each binder normally contains five panels with a capacity of 40 fiche each. The pockets usually have wide cut-outs on both sides to make it easy to remove and insert fiche. Good quality panels are made of durable plastic that is totally compatible with the composition of microfiche. Insertable index strips can be used to facilitate identification of fiche. The binders, when full with 200 microfiche, will be about the same size as a bound journal and can be placed on conventional library shelving. Also available are easel binders which can be opened and propped up to display the fiche headers. They would be most suitable for a frequently used reference collection which is kept on a separate table such as PHONEFICHE.

Ring King Visibles microfiche storage panel.

Eichner easel binder for microfiche.

Eichner fiche storage system.

Taylor-Merchant microfiche rotary stand.

The panels which fit the binders may also be suspended in a rotary stand similar to the periodical finding files used in many libraries until computer-produced holdings lists became popular. Some units hold as many as 100 panels or up to 4,400 fiche. By attaching suspension hooks the panels may be suspended in any file cabinet drawer rack with the indexing channel remaining fully visible. Desk stands or wall systems are also available.

Desk-top trays are also very good for the constant daily use of the same fiche. The typical tray has a capacity of 1,000 fiche without envelopes. Some libraries have found they are very good for placing annual reports of corporations or other heavily used titles on microfiche out by a machine or cluster of machines. Some companies market "touch-fan" files to make it possible to browse through a fiche file and separate the fiche at any point for quick removal and subsequent refiling. Magnets and plastic dividers are used to accomplish this. Desk-top trays should be vacuumed out regularly and fiche should be cleaned more regularly than that kept in storage cabinets.

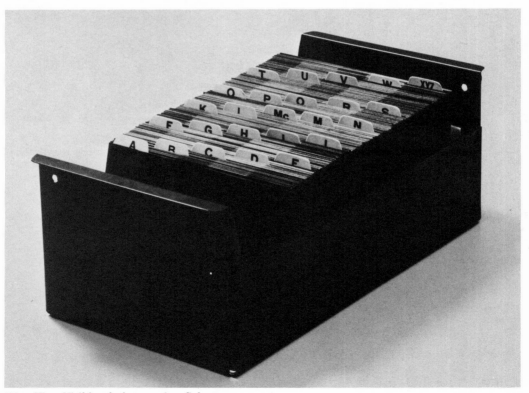

Ring King Visibles desk-top microfiche tray.

Visu-Flex Microfiche Touch-Fan File.

Rolodex Fiche-V-File storage system.

A system called Retrix is available for libraries which wish to file fiche randomly and retrieve them quickly. The fiche are inserted into clear plastic holders which are suspended from a heavy plastic suspension strip. A five digit code is notched into the suspension strip identifying the item by serial or code number. The holder with the fiche inside may then be inserted at random into any one of several size cabinets. When one wishes to retrieve a fiche, a mechanical selector bar which moves along the top of each storage drawer or compartment is coded with the index number. The selector bar is then moved along a guide rail to the left and back to raise the desired holder.

TDC Retrix Random Fiche System (Courtesy: Terminal Data Corporation).

Steel storage cabinets are the most desirable
method of storage because of the protection they afford
from particulate air contaminants and dust.   Floor
cabinets are the most cost effective for long-term high
capacity storage.   The capacities vary a great deal,
not only because of differences in exterior dimensions,
but also differences in utilization of interior space.
The average cabinet used in libraries stores 16,000 to
30,000 fiche without envelopes, but some accommodate
over 90,000.   The cabinet which stores 90,000 fiche is
a 10 drawer unit which is 42 inches wide and only 28
inches deep.   It is a good idea to divide the price of

Russ Bassett fiche storage cabinets.

a cabinet by the capacity in number of fiche to get the per fiche storage cost. Then one can compare different cabinets and determine which is in fact the least expensive unit. A simple alternative to this formula is to divide the price of a cabinet by the number of thousands of fiche it holds.

Business and industry use motorized files for automatic selection of fiche. Some units merely recall a specific tray while others recall a specific fiche. The former type may house up to 300,000 fiche. The largest, most sophisticated fiche storage and retrieval system is ARMS (Automated Records Management System), a product of Teknekron Inc. From any number

of remote high resolution terminals the user can
automatically select a microfiche document and see the
video image in less than five seconds. The centrally
located fiche file is automatically controlled by an
index computer allowing random accesses to as many as
30 million pages of text on fiche. The fiche are
actually stored in large carrousels similar to slide
carrousels. A basic system starts at approximately
$250,000 so the application can be considered only by
very large libraries or by consortia that wish to share
a fiche collection.

Roll Film Cabinets:

Most libraries which purchase storage cabinets for
their 16 or 35mm microfilm purchase 8 to 11 drawer
(horizontally installed) cabinets which have five equal
compartments per drawer, each extending from front to
back. A typical 8 drawer cabinet may house 1,100 16mm
rolls or 650 35mm rolls. An 11 drawer cabinet of the
same width and depth will normally house 1,500 16mm
rolls or 900 35mm rolls. In order to realize greater
floor space utilization when necessary, the units
should be obtained from a manufacturer which also
produces companion cabinets which fit piggy-back on top
the floor units. The companion units normally have
five drawers which are vertically installed. The total
heighth of an 11 drawer floor model cabinet with
companion unit is usually not more than 90 inches. The
addition of the companion unit will give a library an
additional storage capacity of 750 or so rolls of 16mm
film or 450 rolls of 35mm film.

Optimum film storage solution at State University of New York-Stony Brook (Photograph by Dave Morrison).

Russ Bassett film storage cabinets using same basic cabinetry as fiche storage.

Storage cabinets are particularly desirable in areas which are very dusty or which are subject to dramatic changes in environment. For libraries which are concerned about the security of collections, storage cabinets are available with locks. It is possible to lock up all of the collection when the area is not staffed or only specified portions which are deemed to be vulnerable to handling without assistance.

Storage cabinets come in a wide variety of colors. The authors recommend that the microform area be enlivened by selecting a color or colors other than the all-too-common green and gray.

Information Design Products alternative to microfilm cabinet storage.

Bookstacks:

Conventional bookstacks continue to be one of the most common storage devices for microform. While often a choice dictated by limited budgets and the fact that bookstacks are frequently already available, they can be put to effective use.

Conventional bookstacks are designed to house materials which are normally from 6 to 10 inches in depth. When using such stacks a library has several options, including shelving the reels side by side like books. Twenty 35mm or forty 16mm reels of microfilm can be stored on a shelf. Bookstacks are not very efficient for shelving reels of roll film one deep when the ranges are placed at standard intervals such as 4'4" from center of range to center of range so many libraries shelve reels two deep, thus doubling the capacity. This makes it more difficult to retrieve materials and maintain filing integrity. Heavily used titles might best be shelved one deep and lesser used titles two deep.

Another alternative is stacking the reels three or four high and one or two deep. This conserves space, but it is a poor way of filing any but infrequently used materials to which only staff have access.

An excellent space-utilization solution is to store 6 or more reels in an acid-free storage box with a cover. This allows the library to use the full depth

Packing conventional bookstacks is suitable only for little-used films.

Highsmith microfilm storage boxes (Courtesy: The Highsmith Co., Inc.).

of each shelf. While this provides for effective storage and offers the roll film considerable protection from dust, browsing and retrieval of roll film stored in boxes is slower than with cabinet storage.

A few libraries have maximized the capacity of conventional bookstacks by installing 12 inch shelves. This makes it possible to place the six-reel storage boxes two deep. This means 48 35mm reels per shelf. At up to 13 shelves per **three foo**t section, the capacity is impressive, although the access is very slow.

Electro-mechanical compact or "mobile" storage systems are also becoming popular, expecially for closed stack collections. The aisles between the stacks can be closed up when not in use because the

Princeton Microfilm's microfilm storage boxes.

stacks move on tracks perpendicular to their length. Since one aisle may serve as many as a dozen ranges of stacks, only a limited number of people can have access to the materials at any one time. By using storage boxes for the microform, the full depth of each shelf can be utilized, thereby storing approximately 43,000 reels of 35mm microfilm in 300 square feet of floor space.

Open versus Closed Stacks:

Librarians appear to be divided about the need to restrict access to microform. The authors have experienced no difficulty in giving patrons direct

Electro-mechanical Compact Storage by Lundia Corporation at Michigan State University.

access to the collections provided oversight of the
area were good--not to prevent theft, but to prevent
refiling by inexperienced users and to help those who
are having difficulty.

Bookstacks are also used effectively by libraries
which interfile all materials regardless of format.
While this does not make as effective use of storage
space, it is a way of promoting the use of microform.
It is most suitable in libraries which have only
limited microform collections.

Aisle space in open access collections must be
more generous than in restricted access areas. No less

Interfiled fiche using fiche panels in binders (Courtesy: University of Guelph).

Interfiling microfilm using film storage boxes at the University of Guelph.

than 32 inch aisles should be provided in open stack
areas. Even more space should be provided between
storage cabinets because it must be possible to pull
out the drawer and still let someone else pass. If the
drawer is 18 inches deep, the aisle must be at least 50
inches.

Planning for the Future:

The final factor to be considered in the selection
of microform storage is the way in which the collection
is changing. It is readily apparent that libraries
have experienced a phenomenal growth in their holdings
of microform, but less obvious and equally important is
the fact that the nature of the collections has been
changing. Many library microform collections are no
longer limited to dissertations, newspapers, and
esoteric research materials. Indeed, most have
developed to the point where indexes and abstracts,
government documents, telephone directories, annual
reports of corporations, and large backfiles of
journals are on microform. Once viewed as little used
materials of some historical value, the library
microform collection in the future will include
materials which will be in considerable demand. These
microform will have to be stored in equipment from
which it can be quickly retrieved.

VI
Training and Orientation

TRAINING AND ORIENTATION

In discussing the development of microform reading facilities, the authors sought to identify and explore several factors which individually and collectively influence the success of a library's microform program. All of these factors together-- pleasant, commodious facilities; equipment that is both serviceable and well maintained; the provision of proper storage; and an aesthetic environment--will not necessarily insure the successful integration of microform in a library. Ultimately, the success or failure of the microform unit rests with the staff, for it is they who serve as the link between the user and the medium.

In talking about staffing and training consider-ations, it is important to stress that it is the admin-istration and staff attitude toward microform throughout the entire library that will affect user reactions. A library administration that publicly advocates the acquisition and use of microform and encourages use by providing adequate human and financial resources can be a significant positive factor. Even more important is a positive attitude on the part of those who are in the position of referring library users to the microform unit. A reference librarian's statement: "I'm sorry, it's on microform" can prejudice a potential first-time user and put the microform staff at a terrible disadvantage when the individual comes to them.

All library staff, professional and support, should be able to use microform equipment, but those who work in the microform area should be particularly adept. An enthusiastic, well trained microform staff, readily accessible to the patrons and able to help them use equipment and various microform materials is absolutely essential to a successful microform facility.

Administrative Responsibility:

The level and composition of staffing will, of course, vary from one institution to another depending on local needs and constraints, as well as the size of the collection and the extent to which it is being used. In any situation, the responsibility for administering the microform area and training the staff should be with a staff member who is a microform specialist and who has a strong interest in training others. In addition to good interpersonal skills, the individual should have the ability to promote the microform medium in creative ways. Ideally the person should have some administrative experience and feel comfortable with electronic and mechanical equipment.

There are few such persons available, but a willing librarian can become such a specialist by an intense program of library school courses, reading, visiting of other libraries, and hands-on use of materials and equipment. Any library which establishes such a position must also be willing to provide the librarian with the time and resources to develop the skills necessary to effectively manage the microform facility.

Less than 20% of the ALA accredited library school programs offer courses in applied micrographics. Should one or more courses be available at a nearby library school, the new microform specialist should attend them. Participation in some of the workshops and conferences offered by the American Library Association and National Micrographics Association would also be highly desirable, not only for the presentations, but for the opportunity to meet other microform specialists. The Annual Microform Conference sponsored by Microform Review is usually an excellent introduction. Extensive reading is imperative. The reader by Albert J. Diaz entitled Microforms in Libraries[16] is a good beginning. The most relevant experience will come from doing. On-the-job training should never be undertaken in ignorance, however, thus the emphasis on other preparation.

If the specialist cannot be assigned full-time, a part-time specialist should be designated and a well-trained support staff person should be assigned to the area. That person will need one or more full-time or part-time assistants depending on the size of the

---

[16] Diaz, Albert J. Microforms in Libraries: A Reader. Weston, CT: Microform Review Inc., 197-

collection and the number of users served. Collections
with over 1 million microform units and as many as 200
users a day can be effectively operated with only one
to three persons on duty at a time, if everyone is well
trained.

Developing a Local Training Program:

Training is a matter of effectively teaching
people what they need to know in order to properly
carry out their job responsibilities. The specialist
will not be able to teach the staff everything that
he/she knows. The specialist must, therefore,
concentrate on that training that is necessary for
effective performance by the staff. By providing an
opportunity for individual staff members to learn
beyond the basic requirements of their jobs, an
incentive for growth can be provided. This might be
done by offering special training sessions beyond the
mandatory ones.

All training that is not mandatory should be
specific to the microform unit so that there will be a
direct benefit to the users of the facility. David
Dowell gave this wise counsel:

"Libraries do not exist to provide training
and development for their staff members, but
rather to provide services to their clients.
Staff training and development should never
become an end in itself. There is little reason
to believe that the most trained and developed

staff is the most productive staff unless there is a strong correlation between the areas of the training and development and the areas of competence needed to perform work assignments."[17]

Approaches to Training:

There are two basic approaches to training, an as-needed basis and a formal training program. In the case of the former, the supervisor observes staff performances and corrects mistakes in procedure and technique as they occur. Training is also given in response to staff questions. Formal training involves the design of a comprehensive program which anticipates all of the elements which may need to be known by the staff member. The first type of training exists in almost all situations, even when the supervisor is not conscious of it. The latter is still uncommon, but the microform facilities which are using this approach appear to have superior public service.

There are three elements in both types of training: (1) the application of personal experience in the development of others, (2) the ability to adjust the training to the individual and (3) a respect for what others can contribute to the training process.

---

[17]Dowell, David R. "The Role of the Supervisor in Training and Staff Development." in Rolland E., Stevens, ed. Supervision of Employees in Libraries. Urbana: University of Illinois Graduate School of Library Science, 2979, p. 59.

Actual situations drawn from past experience are more
compelling than stated principles. They help people to
remember. Not all staff members learn equally quickly
or in the same way, however, so a variety of training
techniques should be employed. If a staff member is
particularly adept at something, he/she ought to be
encouraged to teach others that skill.

The authors strongly recommend a formal training
program, even for small microform units with less than
five full and part-time staff members. In fact, it is
staff in small units that require the broadest possible
training. The training program should first be
planned, then implemented, and finally evaluated.

Planning:

It is in this phase that one decides who shall do
the training. It will normally be the microform
specialist. If that person is not a capable trainer,
he/she might seek the help of another person within or
without the microform unit. After the "who" question
is answered, it is necessary to determine "what" will
be taught and the extent of the teaching. Questions of
content, length, and frequency should be decided. One
should decide whether to train only the staff of the
unit or others from outside the unit as well. When and
where can the training be performed? What money is
available to perform the training?

By preparing an outline of the training program's

content it is possible to determine whether there is a logical sequence and to set the relative priority of each of the components. A variety of training techniques should be incorporated. Training which consists of one person standing in front of a group talking continuously has been demonstrated to be very ineffective. Some trainers are excellent role players --if so, that skill should be exploited. Demonstrations are good only if some hands-on experience is offered those being trained. A checklist of techniques to be considered should include:

- o Lecture
- o Discussion
- o Role playing
- o Exhibit
- o Audio-visuals
- o Demonstration
- o Games
- o Case study
- o Pre-packaged courses
- o Off-site workshops
- o Job rotation
- o Observation and correction
- o Assigned reading

In addition to training in the manual skills of equipment use, the training should emphasize that microform is a normal, integral part of the library's resources and not something unusual.

Training should not be a one-time affair, but ongoing. The planning should include provision for follow-up to the initial training. There should be provision for those trained to demonstrate their skills to the supervisor or trainer. There should be a

detailed staff training manual for consultation. It
should spell out both the policies and procedures
relevant to the microform area.

Implementatation:

The next step after planning the program is the
implementation. There are a number of do's and don'ts
to keep in mind:

- o Don't crowd too much into one session
- o Do encourage discussion
- o Don't cut off discussion which can lead to
  clarifying questions
- o Do provide immediate correction when needed
- o Don't expect a high level of absorption
- o Do provide clear descriptions
- o Don't forget to combine recognition with
  instruction
- o Do provide immediate trial if possible
- o Don't exhibit impatience
- o Do honestly admit when something is difficult or
  unpleasant

Most important of all, one should explain the purpose
of the training--more than once.

Evaluation:

The purpose of evaluation is to improve the
training program. One is concerned that the training
is improving knowledge, attitudes, and on-the-job
effectiveness in dealing with users. There are at
least four methods of evaluation which might be used:

1) Observation--by watching the actual performance
of staff and the reactions of users to them one can

ascertain whether the staff is accomplishing what was intended.

2) Performance demonstration--by asking staff to demonstrate operation of equipment or other skills so that the trainer can determine that these have been mastered.

3) Testing--by applying written tests one can determine whether staff have acquired the necessary knowledge.

4) Feed-back--by seeking staff reaction, preferably anonymously, the trainer can determine how staff feel about the training they have received.

A Sample Training Program:

One academic library which uses a large number of student assistants has developed a training program around a manual[18] which has since been used by a number of other libraries to develop their training programs. While the manual emphasizes the training of student staff it is usable in many environments. The manual is divided into twelve parts, each of which provides specific information about the library and its microform unit, known as the Microforms Division, and basic micrographics. There are articles and pamphlets on various aspects of micrographics included.

---

[18]Princeton University Library. "Student Assistants Training Manual," (unpublished) 1978.

The "Student Assistant Training Manual," commonly called the SATM, has an introduction, a part describing the library, one on the Microforms Division, an entire part on the role and duties of student assistants, another explaining the card catalog, and a series of parts on microform, microform equipment, circulation, reshelving, the microform collection, and security/closing procedures. A final part provides a large number of miscellaneous details.

Upon first reading, the amount and type of training may seem excessive, but keep in mind that a person who has limited competence with materials or machines is apt to be a self-conscious and reluctant teacher of others. A poorly instructed user is likely to be frustrated.

In summary the training program, of which the SATM is a central part, provides:

Initial Orientation:

Entire student assistant staff:

A group meeting is held at the beginning of the semester for all student assistants during which the following are covered:
1. Introduction of new staff members
2. Brief discussion of the Library and the purpose and objectives of the Microforms Division.
3. Outline of the responsibilities of each student assistant
4. Schedule assignments.
5. New students are shown a slide/tape program

Returning student assistant staff:

1. The librarian works with each returning student assistant individually to go over changes since previous employment. The staff member is then reminded of equipment use and care, the location of materials, etc.
2. The staff member then takes a short oral quiz on the above.
3. The staff member is asked to locate 20 items representative of a cross section of all forms of material.
4. The staff member demonstrates the use of each different piece of equipment.

Training of new staff:

Each new staff member undergoes 3-4 four hour training sessions with the microform specialist during which both theoretical information and practical instruction are given. The training is built around the manual, a slide/tape program and other home-made training aids. The training is divided into three sessions:

Session I:
1. Presentation on the importance of good public service.
2. Briefing on specific responsibilities.
3. Instructions on completing pay vouchers.
4. Walking tour of facility.
5. Overview of locations of equipment, materials and supplies.
6. Briefing on statistics keeping.
7. Telephone manners are discussed.
8. Reading of Parts I to IV of manual.
9. Question and answer period for above.
10. Reading of Part V of manual.
11. Quiz on use of the card catalog
12. Exercise in putting 200 circulation cards in call number order.

Session II:
1. Exercise in finding 20 citations in the Public Catalog.
2. Reading of Parts VI and VII of the manual.
3. Demonstration of each equipment type and hands-on practice.
4. Detailed explanation of the location and variations in call numbers for each type of microform.
5. Reading of Part VIII of the manual.
6. Briefing on recording of reshelving statistics.
7. Exercise putting 75 reels of microfilm in call number order.
8. Reshelving of above reels under observation.
9. Participation in evening area closing procedure.

Session III:
1. Exercise locating 75 items representative of a cross section of all forms of materials.
2. Staff member to demonstrate use of each type of equipment and explain any quirks they may have.
3. Exercise shelving several reels of microfilm under observation.
4. Staff member performs evening closing procedure under observation.

After ascertaining that the staff member has a command of all of the elements of operating the microform area and that he/she is comfortable with being left alone, the staff member is assigned a regular schedule. Some of the hours may be worked alone. After the first three weeks of working alone, an oral test is administered. Assuming satisfactory results, the staff member is considered to be trained. If the results are not satisfactory, more training may be given or the person reassigned or terminated.

Full-time personnel are given the same training program as part-time personnel, but usually in far greater detail. The training also extends to the changing of paper, replacing of lamps, and adjustment of cables. Training in the use of reference tools is also an important part of the preparation of a full-time staff member.

Library Staff of Other Areas:

All new library employees and other interested staff members are formally introduced to the Microforms Division during a 90 minute seminar which is part of the library-wide staff development program. A 20 minute slide/tape presentation covers the various formats, equipment, bibliographic access, and the scope of the collection. A 20-30 minute discussion period follows. The reasons why the library acquires materials in microform are discussed at this time. A tour of the unit is given, including a demonstration of equipment. Seminar participants are encouraged to retrieve microform and use it on the equipment.

Developing a Local Staff Training Program:

Every library's training program will have to reflect its unique needs and resources. The time invested in training should be as much as a library can afford because good staff training does appear to result in greater user success. There appears to be another benefit: staff turnover appears to be less when

people are extensively trained and they know their jobs
well.

<u>Teaching the User</u>:

The principal differences between teaching the
library patron to operate microform equipment and
training the staff about them are that the patron does
not need to be taught to clean and maintain the
equipment and the patron should be offered substantial
control over the amount of training given. Both patron
and staff member need to learn to become competent
machine operators. In addition, the staff member must
be able to teach the patron at the pace and to the
extent the patron appears to want. The latter point
must be stressed, because libraries with training
programs for users sometimes overdo it. If a patron
has only a few minutes for a quick look-up of
information, a detailed equipment review will result in
a negative response.

In addition to adjusting to the patron, the staff
member must not leave the impression that microform is
a fragile medium which the patron may destroy with a
single mistake. Staff should state in a matter of fact
way that some damage is expected and that the help of
the patron is solicited in identifying damage that has
occurred so that it may be repaired, not so that
someone can be made to pay for it.

No matter how well-staffed a microform area is and

how well trained each person, some patrons will be
fending for themselves. It is important to put clear
identification and operating instructions on each
machine. One of the authors recalls his own
embarrassment when taking a visitor to what he believed
was a fiche machine to show off some color fiche. The
machine was an opaque reader which looked at first
glance like some fiche readers.

General User Orientation:

Group tours for library patrons are a natural form
of user orientation, but unless the groups are small it
is difficult to hold the attention of everyone. Some
libraries use film-loops, slide/tape programs, or video
tape demonstrations. Librarians with whom we have
spoken believe that bulletin boards and displays are
equally effective, however, and require a smaller
investment of time. One library features a "Fiche of
the Month" and "Read...on Film" and has not only
increased use of the materials featured, but increased
use of microform in general. Displays in principal
exhibit cases require more work, but make it possible
to combine books, microforms, and other objects in
attention getting ways. A one-page hand-out describing
the microform area placed in books charged out from the
general circulation desk also appears to be effective.
The librarians who have used these techniques consider
them more than publicity. The materials are designed
to inform patrons about when and how to use the
microform area. They are, therefore, part of the
orientation program.

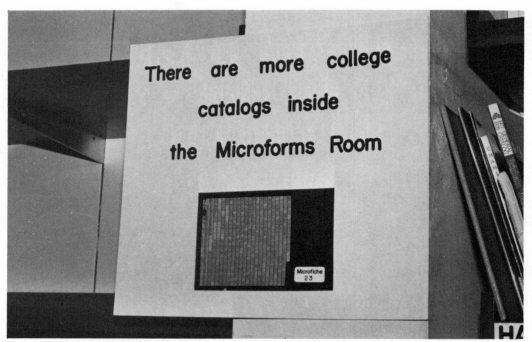

University of Massachusetts microforms promotional sign.

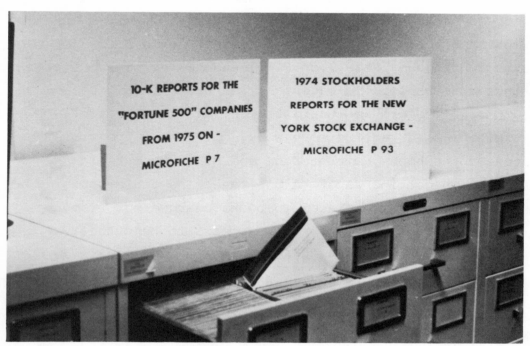

Clear instructions at Denver University.

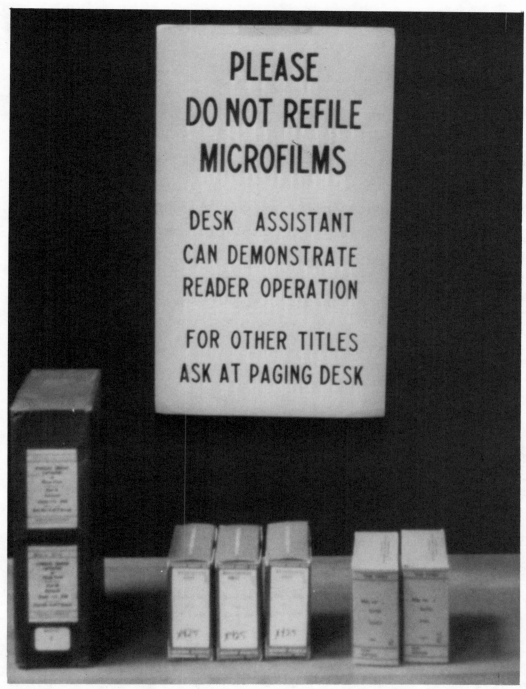

University of Michigan sign orienting users.

Graphics:

The authors have visited more than 50 microform facilities in the past three years. We are convinced that good graphics or signage plays an important role in drawing people into a microform area and in orienting them after they get there. A complete graphics system includes markings on all stack ranges and storage cabinets (not just call numbers, but also the names of frequently used publications such as the Wall Street Journal), labels on all microform storage boxes, identification of each piece of equipment as to its function, operational instructions and diagrams, and a good floor plan of any but the very smallest microform facility.

Prominent graphics at SUNY-Stony Brook.

Graphics in the Denver University Library microforms area.

Stacks graphics at Michigan State University.

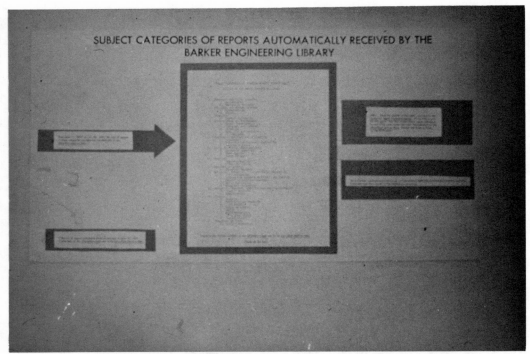

MIT Barker Engineering Library display.

Conclusion:

Few libraries have a formal training program such as that described in this chapter. Even fewer have user orientation programs and planned graphics. Informal training on an as-needed basis is the rule and users usually have to fend for themselves much of the time. But then, most libraries also lack good facilities at this time. The authors believe that as microform becomes a more important part of libraries' collections it will become more and more necessary to formalize the staff training and user orientation or there will be widespread user dissatisfaction. It has in the past been possible for most users to avoid microform, but this will probably not be the case in the future. Microform will play an increasing role in every type of library as deteriorating book papers force more preservation microfilming on us, as space pressures make the microform more attractive, and as more publishers choose microform as an original publication medium.

VII
Conclusion

CONCLUSION

In this book we have emphasized that libraries should not commit tens-of-thousands or hundreds-of-thousands of dollars to the acquisition of books, journals and other publications in microform without carefully planning the facilities and staffing.

No one element in the planning can be neglected because all are interrelated. An attractive reading area provides a good first impression, but unsuitable equipment will shortly change that impression. High quality equipment that is poorly maintained will leave a much worse impression than well-maintained inexpensive equipment. Finally, a competent, enthusiastic staff is necessary to orient and assist users.

Is the Effort Worthwhile?

Some librarians have asked us whether all of this effort is worthwhile in light of the development of video disk as a storage medium. They have heard that this new medium will displace microform within the next few years. The effort is worthwhile because it will, in our opinion, take several years for video disk to be widely adopted, and when it is libraries will augment their microform collections with video disk, rather than replace their existing collections.

Video disk has the advantage of very dense storage. Nearly 110,000 images or frames can be stored on a single optical video disk the size of a long-playing phonograph record. Each disk contains less than $.50 worth of plastic. Individual frames can be accessed in seconds. There are some constraints on the medium, however.

Constraints on Video Disk:

There are a number of reasons why microform publishers and others will not begin using video disk technology in the near future, among them:

(1) The preparation of material prior to the manufacturing of a master video disk from which copies can be stamped is slow and costly.

(2) The stamping equipment is exceedingly expensive. Only one production size stamping facility existed in the United States in early 1981.

(3) The manufacturing of a video disk is presently cost effective only when at least 2,000 copies are to be made from a single master.

(4) The present state of the art allows high quality reproduction of pictures, but the reproduction of printed text has not yet been perfected.

(5) There are competing optical video disk technologies on the market. No one knows which of the imcompatible systems will succeed and which will fail. Making a decision now is, therefore, quite risky.

(6) Microform publishers often have restricted reproduction rights. They may have contractual

commitments which authorize them to microfilm or to make any type of microform reproduction, but a video disk edition would have to be newly negotiated.

(7) The large majority of microform publishers lack the capital to change from one medium to another.

The diffusion rate of any technology is slow. Long after a new technology is perfected and becomes economically feasible, it remains unpopular with those who have a vested interest in continuing to use existing technologies.

If one looks back, it is clear that libraries seldom abandon old technologies if they have invested a considerable amount of money in collections which remain usable. The materials on microform now in libraries will remain just as useful as those which are in printed form. Just as libraries have undertaken only limited conversion of existing hard-copy collections to microform, they will probably undertake only limited conversion of microform to video disk. Libraries prefer to commit their limited resources to the acquisition of new titles.

The Digital Video Disk:

It is our view that the optical video disk now reaching the market will not be the disk on which large quantities of information will be stored. A digital video disk with a much higher storage capacity has already been developed. Called the digital video disk or the digital disk, it stores information in machine-readable form rather than as frames. One laboratory is experimenting with a disk which can store 5 billion characters and there are predictions that a 10 billion character digital disk will be developed soon. The incredible storage capacity of a digital disk can best be illustrated by comparing it to the 30 volume Encyclopedia Americana which contains approximately 150 million characters.

If microform publishers and others move to the digital disk without using the optical video disk as an interim step, it may be a decade before libraries will have a significant number of titles available in the new format. During that time microform will continue to be the dominant non-print medium.

Appendices

A. Bibliography
B. Glossary

BIBLIOGRAPHY

I. General Works--Monographs:

American Library Association. Resources and Technical
    Services Division. Library Standards for
    Microfilm Committee. Microfilm Norms: Recommended
    Standards for Libraries. Chicago, IL: ALA, 1966.

Avedon, Don M. Introduction to Micrographics. Silver
    Spring, MD: National Microfilm Association, 1973.

Ballou, Hubbard, ed. Guide to Microreproduction
    Equipment. 5th ed. Annapolis, MD, National
    Microfilm Association, 1971; 1972 supplement.

Bernhardt, Homer I. An Overview of Microforms: A
    Report on the Role of Microforms in the University
    of Pittsburgh Libraries. Pittsburg, PA: The
    University, 1972.

Costigan, Daniel M. Micrographic Systems. Silver
    Spring, MD: National Microfilm Association,
    1975.
Diaz, Albert J. Microforms in Libraries: A Reader.
    Westport, CT: Microform Review, 1975.

Dranov, Paul. Microfilm: The Librarians' View,
    1976-77. White Plains, NY: Knowledge Industry
    Publications, 1976.

Fair, Judy. Microforms Management in Special
    Libraries: A Reader. Westport, CT: Microform
    Review, 1979.

Gabriel, Michael R. and Roselle, William C. The
    Microform Revolution in Libraries, vol. 3.
    Greenwich, CT: JAI Press, 1980.

Gordon, Ronald F. 16mm Microfilm Viewing Equipment
    Guide. Alexandria, VA: Defense Documentation
    Center, 1971.

Hawken, William R. Evaluating Microfiche Readers: A
     Handbook for Librarians. Washington DC: Council
     on Library Resources, 1975.

Holmes, Donald C. Determination of the Environmental
     Conditions Required in a Library for the Effective
     Utilization of Microforms. Interim Report.
     Washington DC: Association of Research Libraries,
     1970 [ED046-403].

_____. Determination of User Needs and Future
     Requirements for A Systems Approach to Microform
     Technology. Washington DC: Association of
     Research Libraries, 1969 [ED029-168].

Morrison, Alta Bradley, ed. MICROFORM UTILIZATION: THE
     ACADEMIC LIBRARY ENVIRONMENT. Report of a
     Conference held at Denver, CO, Dec. 7-9, 1970,
     Denver, CO: University of Denver, 1971.

New, Peter G. Repography for Librarians. Hamden, CT:
     Linnet Books, 1975.

Rice, E. Stevens. FICHE AND REEL, rev. ed. Ann Arbor,
     MI: Xerox University Microfilms, 1972.

Saffady, William. MICROGRAPHICS. Littleton, CO:
     Libraries Unlimited, 1978.

Smith, Virginia Carlson. "Microforms" (Ch. 15) in
     Pacey, Philip. ART LIBRARY MANUAL: A GUIDE TO
     RESOURCES AND PRACTICES. New York: Bowker, 1972,
     pp. 236-55.

Spencer, Herbert, and Reynolds, Linda. FACTORS
     AFFECTING THE ACCEPTABILITY OF MICROFORMS AS A
     READING MEDIUM. London: Royal College of Art.
     Readability of Print Research Unit, 1976.

Spigai, Frances G. THE INVISIBLE MEDIUM: THE STATE OF
     THE ART OF MICROFORM AND A GUIDE TO THE
     LITERATURE. Stanford, CA: ERIC Clearinghouse on
     Media and Technology, 1973.

Teague, S. J. MICROFORM LIBRARIANSHIP, 2nd ed. Woburn,
     MA: Butterworths, 1979.

U.S. General Services Administration. National
Archives and Records Service. Office of Records
Management. RECORDS MANAGEMENT HANDBOOK:
MICROFORM RETRIEVAL EQUIPMENT GUIDE. Washington,
D.C.: Office of Records Management, 1970.

Veaner, Allen B. THE EVALUATION OF MICROPUBLICATIONS.
Chicago, IL: ALA, 1971. (Library Technology
Program Publication No. 17).

II. General Works: Periodical Articles:

Ashby, Peter. "On Becoming Microminded: An Incitement
to Thought on the Subject of Microfilm in
Libraries." LIBRARY ASSOCIATION RECORD 77(9)
September 1975: 214-15+.

Asleson, Robert F. "Microforms: Where Do they Fit?"
LIBRARY RESOURCES AND TECHNICAL SERVICES 15(1)
Winter 1971: 57-66.

Becker, Joseph. "Review of Microforms: Preliminary
Remarks/General Discussion," in Conference on
Libraries and Automation--Airlie Foundation,
1963. Washington DC: Library of Congress, 1964,
pp. 143-51.

Bell, Jo Ann. "Microforms: Uses and Potential."
MEDICAL LIBRARY ASSOCIATION BULLETIN 66(2) April
1978: 232-38.

Blank, John B. "Managing Library Microform Resources
in the 1980's." AMERICAN SOCIETY FOR INFORMATION
SCIENCE PROCEEDINGS, vol. 14, 1977. White Plains:
Knowledge Industry Publications, 1978.

Davies, J. Eric. "Microforms in Libraries: A
Description and Some Observations." IATUL
PROCEEDINGS 10 (1978): 13-31.

Doebler, Paul. "Coping with Microforms in Libraries."
PUBLISHERS WEEKLY 208(19) Nov. 10, 1975: 30.

_____. "Libraries on Microfiche: LRI's Experience
in the Field." PUBLISHERS WEEKLY 202(25) Dec. 18,
1972: 27-30.

"Guidelines for the Handling of Microforms in the Yale
    University Library," MICROFORM REVIEW 9(1) Winter
    1980: 11-20; 9(2) Spring 1980: 72-85.

Hawken, William R. "Making Big Ones Out of Little
    Ones" (Current Trends in Micrographics). LIBRARY
    JOURNAL 102(13) Oct. 15, 1977: 2127-31.

Hess, Edward J. "It's Time for a Positive Approach to
    Micro-Graphics." LAW LIBRARY JOURNAL 64(2) May
    1971: 176-83.

Kiersky, Loretta J. "Which Microform? Which System?"
    THE RUB-OFF 19(1) Jan.-Feb. 1968: 1-4.

MacDonald, Eric; Eichhorn, Sara, and Phelps, Roberta.
    "A Survey of Current Microform Practices in
    California Libraries." MICROFORM REVIEW 7(3)
    May/June 1978: 146-60.

Malinconico, S. Michael. "The Display Medium." LIBRARY
    JOURNAL 101(18) Oct. 15, 1976:2144-49.

Meadow, Charles T. "Microfilm and the Library: A
    Perspective." DREXEL LIBRARY QUARTERLY 11(4)
    Oct. 1975: 83-8.

"Microforms--Problems and Prospects." [Extracted from
    "Microfiche, Microfilm, and Hard Copy--Problems
    and Prospects for the Research Worker" by William
    R. Hawken in NATIONAL MICRO-NEWS, Dec. 1964:
    106-7.] SPECIAL LIBRARIES 56(10) Dec. 1965: 730.

Phillips, William F. "Microforms in the Library."
    FOCUS ON INDIANA LIBRARIES 23(1) March 1969:
    14-16.

Simmons, R.A. "Microforms and the Library."
    AUSTRALIAN LIBRARY JOURNAL 22(3) April 1973:
    97-104.

Spaulding, Carl M. "Getting the Most Out of
    Microforms" (35th LSU Library Lecture). (In
    Louisiana State University, Baton Rouge. Graduate
    School of Library Science. LIBRARY LECTURES,
    numbers twenty-nine through thirty-five.
    Louisiana State University Library, 1978, p.
    44-48.

Stevens, Rolland E.   "The Microform Revolution."
     LIBRARY TRENDS 19(3) Jan. 1971:379-95.

Thompson, Lawrence S.   "Microforms Are Not Expendable."
     LIBRARY SECURITY NEWSLETTER 1(3) May/June 1975:11.

Veaner, Allen B.   "Micrographics: An Eventful Forty
     Years--What Next?" in 1976 ALA YEARBOOK, pp.
     45-56.

_____. "Microfilm and the Library: A
     Retrospective." DREXEL LIBRARY QUARTERLY 11(3)
     Oct. 1975: 3-15.

Veit, Fritz.   "Microforms, Microform Equipment and
     Microform Use in the Educational Environment."
     LIBRARY TRENDS 19(4) April 1971: 447-66.

White, Howard S.   "Micrographics," in 1977 ALA
     YEARBOOK, pp. 207-8.

_____. "Micrographics," in 1978 ALA YEARBOOK,
     pp. 188-90.

III.   Microform Reading Rooms

Fair, Judy.   "The Microtext Reading Room," MICROFORM
     REVIEW 1 (3), July 1972: 199-2-2; 1 (4) Oct.
     1972; 2 (1) Jan. 1973;

Fishman, Diane and Walitt, Ruth.   "Seating and Area
     Preferences in a College Reserve Room." COLLEGE
     AND RESEARCH LIBRARIES 33 (4) July 1972: 284-96.

Spreitzer, Francis F.   "Library Microform Facilities.:
     LIBRARY TECHNOLOGY REPORTS 12 (4) July 1976:
     407-35.

Tannenbaum, Arthur C.   "Human Engineering Factors Help
     Determine Microform Use in the Research Library."
     In: "INFORMATION REVOLUTION: PROCEEDINGS OF THE
     38TH ASIS ANNUAL MEETING, vol. 12, 1975. Boston:
     The Association, 1976.

Weber, David C.   "Design for a Microtext Reading Room."
     UNESCO BULLETIN FOR LIBRARIES 20 (6) Nov./Dec.
     1966: 303:08.

IV. Administration

Beck, William L. "A Realistic Approach to Microform
    Management." MICROFORM REVIEW 2(3) July 1973:
    172-6. [+ LISA Abstract]

Carroll, C. Edward. "Some Problems of Microform
    Utilization in Large University Collections."
    MICROFORM REVIEW 1(1) Jan. 1972: 19-24. [+ LISA
    Abstract]

Dodson, Suzanne. "The University of British Columbia's
    Guide to Large Collections in Microform: One
    Attempt to Minimize a Major Problem." MICROFORM
    REVIEW 1(2) April 1972: 113-17.

Farber, Evan Ira. "The Administration and Use of
    Microform Serials in College Libraries."
    MICROFORM REVIEW 7(2) March 1978: 81-4.

Heim, Kathleen M. "The Role of Microforms in the Small
    College Library." MICROFORM REVIEW 3(4) Oct.
    1974: 254-9.

Vandenburgh, Anne. "Inventory of Microform Centers
    on a Major University Campus." MICROFORM REVIEW
    7 (6) Nov. 1978: 317-20.

Veaner, Allen B. "Micropublication," in Voight, Melvin,
    ed. ADVANCES IN LIBRARIANSHIP, vol.2 (1971), pp.
    165-73.

Yerburgh, Mark R. "Academic Libraries and the
    Evaluation of Microform Collections." MICROFORM
    REVIEW 7(1) Jan./Feb. 1978: 14-19.

_____. "Microforms, Staff Development, and the
    Pursuit of Excellence." MICROFORM REVIEW 9(3)
    Summer 1980: 139-44.

V. Education/Training

Kottenstette, James P. "Student Reading Character-
    istics: Comparing Skill-Levels Demonstrated on
    Hardcopy and Microform Presentations." In:
    PROCEEDINGS OF ASIS ANNUAL MEETING, vol. 6 (1969),
    pp. 345-51.

Martin, Murray S.   "Promoting Microforms to Students
     and Faculty." MICROFORM REVIEW 8(2) Spring 1979:
     87-91.

Morrison, Alta Bradley, ed.   MICROFORM UTILIZATION: THE
     ACADEMIC LIBRARY ENVIRONMENT.   Report of a
     Conference held at Denver, CO, Dec. 7-9, 1970,
     Denver, CO: University of Denver, 1971.

Schwarz, Philip John.   "Instruction in the Use of
     Microform Equipment." WISCONSIN LIBRARY BULLETIN
     67(5) Sept./Oct. 1971: 341-43.

_____. "Learning to Use Microform Equipment: A
     Self-Instructional Approach." MICROFORM REVIEW
     4(4) Oct. 1975: 262-5.

Spaulding, Carl M.   "Teaching the Use of Microfilm
     Readers." MICROFORM REVIEW 6(2) Mar. 1977: 80-1.

University Microfilms International.   A MICROCOURSE IN
     MICROFORMS.   Ann Arbor, MI: UMI, 1978. [Reviewed
     by Wm. Saffady in MICROFORM REVIEW 8(1) Winter
     1979: 55-56.]

VI. <u>Reprography</u>

Avedon, Don M.   INTRODUCTION TO MICROGRAPHICS. Silver
     Spring, MD: National Microfilm Association, 1973.

Davis, Jinnie Y.   "Micropublishing in Color: An Answer
     to the Art Publishers Dilemma?" MICROFORM REVIEW
     8 (3) Summer 1979: 193-97.

Hawken, William R.   COPYING METHODS MANUAL. Chicago,
     IL: ALA, Library Technology Program, 1966.

Hayes, Robert M. and Becker, Joseph.   HANDBOOK OF DATA
     PROCESSING FOR LIBRARIANS. New York: Wiley, 1970,

Jestes, Edward C.   "Little Fiche Eat Big Librarians--
     One Whale of a Story." WILSON LIBRARY BULLETIN
     44(6) Feb. 1970: 650-2.

Maxwell, Monty M.   "Unconventional Photographic
     Systems; How Will They Change Your Library?"
     WILSON LIBRARY BULLETIN 46(6) Feb. 1972: 518-24.

New, Peter G. REPROGRAPHY FOR LIBRARIANS. Hamden, CT: Linnet Books, 1975.
Morrison, Alta Bradley, ed.

Ryan, William T. "Blowbacks from Microcards? Here's a Way." SPECIAL LIBRARIES 63 (4) Apr. 1972: 202.

VII. Preservation/Storage:

"ALA Microform Recommendation." AMERICAN ARCHIVIST 39 (2) 1976: 228.

Asleson, Robert F. "Microforms as an Alternative to Building" in "Running Out of Space--What are the Alternatives." Chicago: ALA, 1976, 24-31.

Bechanan, H. Gordon. "The Organization of Microforms in the Library." LIBRARY TRENDS 8 (1959-60): 391-406.

"Care of Microfilm and Microfilm Readers." AMERICAN ARCHIVIST 37 (2) April 1974: 314-15.

Darling, Pamela W. "Developing a Preservation Micro-filming Program." LIBRARY JOURNAL 99 (Nov. 1, 1974): 2803-9.

_____. "Microforms in Libraries: Preservation and Storage." MICROFORM REVIEW 5(2) April 1976: 93-100.

Haverling, Sven-G. "Technical Aspects of the Preservation of Archival (Security) Microfilm." UNESCO BULLETIN FOR LIBRARIES 29 (2) March/April 1975: 68-74+.

Klein, Henry. "Microfilm Resuscitation--A Case Study." JOURNAL OF MICROGRAPHICS 9(6) July 1976: 299-303.

Knight, Nancy H. "Cleaning of Microforms." LIBRARY TECHNOLOGY REPORTS 14 (May 1978: 217-40.

"Microfilm Storage Standards Revised." LAW LIBRARY JOURNAL 68(3) Aug. 1975: 325.

Napier, Paul A. "Film Types: Choices and Problems."
    AMERICAN LIBRARIES 7 (Oct. 1976) 588-89.

Raikes, Deborah A. "Microform Storage in Libraries."
    LIBRARY TECHNOLOGY REPORTS 15(4) July/Aug 1979:
    445-448.

"Recommendations for Storage of Permanent Record
    Microfilm." MICROFORM REVIEW 3(4) Oct. 1974: 248.

Spaulding, Carl M. "Kicking the Silver Habit: Confess-
    ions of a former Addict." JOURNAL OF MICROGRAPH-
    ICS 9(12) December 1978: 653-6.

VIII. Equipment

Ballou, Hubbard, ed. "Guide to Microreproduction
    Equipment" (5th ed) 1971 and supplements. Silver
    Spring, MD: National Micrographics Association.

Hawken, William R. "Evaluating Microfiche Readers: A
    Handbook for Librarians." Washington, D.C.:
    Council on Library Resources, 1975.

Jones, M. L. "User Maintenance of Micrographics
    Equipment." REPROGRAPHICS QUARTERLY 12(3)
    Summer 1979: 84-86.

LaHood, Charles G. Jr. "Selecting and Evaluating
    Microform Reading Equipment for Libraries."
    MICROFORM REVIEW 6(2) Mar. 1977: 79.

Miller, Roger C. "Why Don't They Make Microform
    Machines for Libraries?" MICROFORM REVIEW 2(2)
    Apr. 1973: 91-2.

National Micrographics Association. "Buyer's Guide to
    Microform Equipment, Products and Services." 1971-
    Silver Spring, MD: NMA.

_____. "How to Select a Reader or Reader-
    Printer." Silver Spring, MD: NMA, 1974.

_____. "A Microform Handbook." Silver Spring,

MD: NMA, 1974.

"New Equipment Reviewing Service."   MICROFORM REVIEW
    5(1) Jan. 1976: 8-9.

"Reader-Printers for Libraries." LIBRARY TECHNOLOGY
    REPORTS 15(2) Mar/Apr 1979 entire issue.

Sherman, Alonzo J.   "How to Pick the Best Reader."
    COMPUTER WORLD (Oct 25, 1972) Suppl 2.

Spaulding, Carl M.   "The Fifty Dollar Reading
    Machine...and Other Micromarvels." LIBRARY
    JOURNAL 101 (18) Oct. 15, 1976: 2133-38.

Weber, David C.   "Specifications for a Superior
    Microtext Reading Machine." AMERICAN
    DOCUMENTATION 16(3) July 1965: 246-7.

GLOSSARY

ARCHIVAL FILM--A photographic film of high quality that is suitable for filming and preserving records that have permanent value.

BACKGROUND--The portion of a microform or an original from which it is made that does not include lettering, lines, or other information.

BASE--A transparent plastic material upon which a photographic emulsion or other material may be coated.

CAMERA--A photographic device using an optical system for exposing light-sensitive material.

CAMERA-PROCESSOR--A device which functions both as a camera and as a processor for developing, etc.

CARTRIDGE--A single core container enclosing processed microfilm designed to be put into a reader or reader-printer.

CASSETTE--A container for microfilm which has a double core for loading film into a reader or reader-printer without threading or rewinding.

CINE MODE--The arrangement of images on roll microfilm in which the lines of print are perpendicular to the length of the film. Also known as vertical mode.

COATING--A liquid or gel that can be applied to processed microfilm in a thin transparent coating to protect the film from scratches, fingerprints, etc.

COMIC MODE--The arrangement of images on roll microfilm in which the lines or print are parallel to the length of the film. Also known as horizontal mode.

CONTACT PRINTING--A method for copying in which the raw stock is held in contact with film bearing the image to be copied.

DARKROOM--A room in which all light not safe for unprocessed film can be controlled.

DENSITY--The light-absorbing or light-reflecting characteristics of a photographic image.

DIAZO--Coated films containing sensitized layers composed of diazonium salts that react with chemical compounds or couplers to form azo dye images.

DIRECT-IMAGE FILM--A film that will retain the same polarity as the previous generation or the original material, black for black, white for white, etc.

DOCUMENT--A medium and the information recorded on it, such as a book or a single page.

DOUBLE FRAME--A combination of two horizontal single frames next to one another.

DUO--A method of recording images on each half of the usable width of the microfilm, first on one half in one direction and then on the other half in the other direction.

DUPLEX--A method of recording images from both front and back of a document on roll microfilm in one exposure so that the images appear side by side across the width of the microfilm.

DUPLICATE--A copy of a microform made by contact printing or optical means OR the act of making such copies.

EMULSION--A coating on a film base consisting of light sensitive materials.

ENVELOPE--A piece of chemically inert folded paper for storing individual microfiche.

EXPOSURE--Submitting sensitive materials to light so that the light will act on it.

FAST FILM--A photographic material of high sensitivity to light.

FILM CLEANING--The removal of foreign matter from film by dusting, wiping, cleaning solvents, etc.

FILM SIZE--Film width, generally expressed in millimeters or mm.

FLATS--Two pieces of smooth, highly polished glass used to hold film in cameras, readers, etc.

FOCAL LENGTH--The distance between the focal point and the lens when the optical system is focused to record an object at a great distance.

FOCUS--To adjust the relative positions of the lens and film to obtain the sharpest possible image.

FRAME--That area of the film on which light or radiant energy can fall during a single exposure.

FRONT PROJECTION--The process of forming an optical image on a reflective surface for viewing or photographing such that the projector is on the same side of the receiving surface as the viewer or the camera.

GELATIN--A medium used to hold silver halide crystals in suspension in photographic emulsions or as a protective layer.

GENERATION--One of the successive stages of photographic reproduction of an original. The first generation is the camera film and copies made from that are the second generation.

HALIDE--Any compound of chlorine, iodine, bromine or fluorine and another element. The compound is called a halogen. The silver salts of a halogen are the light-sensitive materials used in silver-halide emulsions.

HEADER--The inscription placed at the top of a microfiche providing the title and other bibliographic information.

HIGH REDUCTION--Reductions of from 1:30 to 1:60 or 30X to 60X.

HOT SPOT--An area on the screen image that appears appreciably lighter than the surrounding areas.

IMAGE--A representation of the information produced by light or radiation.

IMAGE REVERSING FILM--A film which when conventionally processed will reverse the polarity of the original material; i. e. whites from blacks.

JACKET--A flat, transparent, plastic carrier with channels to hold strips of microfilm.

LATENT IMAGE--The invisible images produced by the action of light or radiant energy on a photosenstive material. It is made visible through the developing process.

LEADER--A length of film at the beginning of a roll to facilitate threading without affecting the images on the film.

MAGNIFICATION RATIO--The expression of the relative degree an object is enlarged by an optical instrument.

MICROFICHE--A transparent sheet of film with micro-images arranged in a grid pattern, usually with a header at the top.

MICROFILM--A fine-grain, high resolution film used to record images that have been reduced in size from the original OR a microform consisting of a roll of images on film.

MICROFORM--A form which contains microimages, including microfilm, microfiche, etc.

MICROFORM PRODUCTION--The process of creating a microform from a document or another microform.

MICROGRAPHICS--Techniques associated with the production, handling and use of microforms.

MICRO-OPAQUE--A very small image on a reflective base that is viewed by reflection rather than projection.

NEGATIVE--An image in which the characters appear light against a dark background.

OPAQUE--Characteristic of material which makes it incapable of transmitting visible light; not translucent.

PLANETARY CAMERA--A type of microfilm camera in which the document being photographed and the film remain in a stationary position during the exposure.

POLARITY--The change or retention of the dark to light relationship of an image. When a positive copy is made of a negative microform the polarity is said to have been changed.

POLYESTER--A transparent plastic used as a film base because of its strength, resistance to tearing and relative noninflammability.

PRESSURE PLATE--A flat plate that holds the film in the focal plane for exposure, projection, etc.

PRINT--A reproduction or copy on photographic film or paper OR to produce a copy.

PROCESSOR--A machine that performs the various operations necessary to make microfilm usable, including developing, fixing, washing and drying.

READER--A machine that enlarges microimages for viewing.

READER-PRINTER--A machine that enlarges microimages for viewing and also has the capability of producing hard copies.

REAR PROJECTION--The projection of an image onto a translucent screen from the side opposite to that from which the image is viewed.

RED SPOTS--A microspot formation on silver film caused by improper storage or air pollution. Also called measles, and redox blemishes.

REDUCTION--The amount the original is reduced to create the microimage measured in terms of the corresponding linear dimensions of the two.

REEL--A flanged holder on which processed roll film is wound.

RESOLUTION--The ability of a photographic system to record fine detail.

ROLL MICROFILM--Microfilm that can be put on a reel or spool.

ROTARY CAMERA--A type of microfilm camera that photographs documents while they are being moved by some form of transport mechanism.

SERVICE COMPANY--An organization that is equipped to do microfilming or other micrographic work under contract.

SHEET FILM--A precut rectangle or flexible transparent-base material coated with a photosensitive material; to be distinguished from roll film.

SIMPLEX--A method of recording images in which a single microimage occupies all or a major portion of the width of the microfilm.

SPLICE--A joint made by cementing, welding, or taping two pieces of film together. If there is no overlap, the splice is called a butt splice.

SPLICER--A device for joining strips of photographic film.

STEP-AND-REPEAT CAMERA--A microfilm camera that can expose a series of separate images on an area of film in an orderly pattern, usually rows and columns.

THREADING--Transferring the leading end of the film from the supply spool or cartridge through the rollers, sprockets, etc. of a piece of micrographic equipment to the take-up device.

THROUGHPUT--The rate at which documents can be processed through a microfilm camera.

TRANSLUCENT SCREEN--A reader screen of plastic or treated glass onto which an image is projected.

ULTRAFICHE--Microfiche with images reduced more than 90 times.

VESICULAR FILM--A film in which the light-sensitive component is suspended in a plastic layer. On exposure, optical vesicles or bubbles are created in the layer to form the latent images. Heating the plastic layer makes the latent images visible.

VIDEO DISK--A flat, circular piece of plastic similar to a phonodisk on which audio, video, and digital information may be stored. The data can be scanned by laser or a special stylus and displayed on a television screen.

For a comprehensive glossary of terms see National Micrographics Association Technical Report Number 2-1980 entitled <u>Glossary of Micrographics</u>.

Index